Judaism

NICHOLAS DE LANGE

Oxford   New York

OXFORD UNIVERSITY PRESS

1986

Oxford University Press, Walton Street, Oxford OX2 6DP

Oxford New York Toronto
Delhi Bombay Calcutta Madras Karachi
Kuala Lumpur Singapore Hong Kong Tokyo
Nairobi Dar es Salaam Cape Town
Melbourne Auckland

and associated companies in
Beirut Berlin Ibadan Nicosia

Oxford is a trade mark of Oxford University Press

British Library Cataloguing in Publication Data
de Lange, Nicholas
Judaism.—(OPUS)
1. Judaism——History
I. Title
296'.09   BM155.2
ISBN 0-19-219198-5

Library of Congress Cataloging in Publication Data
de Lange, N. R. M. (Nicholas Robert Michael),
1944–
Judaism.
(OPUS)
Bibliography: p.
Includes index.
1. Judaism.   I. Title.   II. Series.
BM561.D38   1986   296   85-21509
ISBN 0-19-219198-5

Set by Colset Private Ltd.
Printed in Great Britain by
Biddles Ltd.
Guildford and King's Lynn

For
Emmanuel and Catherine

Preface

No one can hope to portray the whole of Judaism, in all its complexity and variety, in the brief compass of a single volume. My object in writing this book has been more limited. For some time I have felt the need of a general book about Judaism which would not be a basic introduction, a popular history, or an apologia. Of such books there is no real shortage. Nor did it seem appropriate to delve deeply into the minutiae of Jewish law or theology or religious observance. This book is intended for the general reader or student who has some basic knowledge, not about Judaism in particular but about religion and history in general. I have tried to explain in a clear and balanced way the foundations on which Judaism rests, and the ways in which it has developed, particularly in the past hundred years or so.

This book is the fruit of many years of teaching and thinking about Judaism. My pupils as well as my own teachers and my colleagues have made their contribution to it. Among so many it would be invidious to attempt to list names. I should like, however, to record my special debt to the late Ignaz Maybaum, at whose feet I sat for some twenty years. From an early age he taught me an appreciation of certain enduring characteristics of Judaism, and of the value of the past in elucidating the present; in particular he made me realize the importance of nineteenth-century Germany for an understanding of contemporary Judaism. At one time we talked of collaborating on a work of Jewish theology: sadly, that book was never written, but perhaps there is something of it in this one.

My thoughts about the contemporary problems facing Judaism were brought into focus by an invitation to participate in an inter-faith consultation at St George's House, Windsor Castle, in 1977; I am grateful to the organizers and participants for giving me that occasion to clarify my ideas. In 1979 I was given an opportunity to explore the concept of tradition in Judaism, which is a central theme of the present book, when I was asked to give a series of lectures as Littman Fellow at the Oxford Centre for Postgraduate Hebrew Studies. This was a valuable experience for me, and I am particularly grateful to Edward Shils for some helpful guidance about the study of tradition at that time.

Two good friends, Isaac Levy and Jonathan Webber, gave proof of their friendship by agreeing to read this book in typescript. I am deeply grateful to them both for their encouraging response and for their judicious and constructive criticisms. To the extent that I did not yield to their suggestions, either through the exigencies of space or through innate stubbornness, the book is less good than it might have been.

NICHOLAS DE LANGE

Cambridge
July 1985

Contents

Introduction: What is Judaism?

The term 'Judaism' is commonly used in a number of different ways. One of the commonest is to refer to a religion, one of the major religions of the world, and a member (together with Christianity and Islam) of what is known as the 'monotheistic family' of religions.

This usage raises several problems, which we shall consider presently, but it is worth beginning by pointing out some of its positive merits.

In the first place it accurately indicates an important historical reality. Judaism, Christianity and Islam do belong together. They all began in the same part of the world, the Middle East. (The honoured place they all ascribe, in their different ways, to the city of Jerusalem is a living reminder of this.) From here they spread out in broadly similar directions. In the specific case of Judaism this historical aspect is particularly important. Since the advent of Christianity and Islam, Judaism has rarely spread, and it has never flourished, beyond the confines of what may be called the Christian-Muslim world. Judaism, Christianity and Islam have developed in close contact with one another, and each religion has influenced the development of the others in important respects. Historically, then, the metaphor of a family is not inappropriate.

Theologically, too, it makes sense to speak of a family relationship. The fundamental beliefs of the three religions are, if not identical, remarkably similar. They all begin from the belief in a single, unique God: this is what we mean by the term 'monotheistic religions'. This God is perfect and incorporeal, the creator of the world and of mankind, existing beyond the world yet active within it. He is just yet compassionate, cares for his creatures and their welfare, makes his will known to mankind through direct revelation, demands and rewards righteousness and punishes wrongdoing. The actual details of the code of behaviour which God demands of man are also very similar in all three religions. Perhaps because of the close family relationship there has been a constant and often hostile internal debate between the three members which has had the effect of bringing to prominence those elements which divide rather than those which unite. But even a superficial comparison between these three religions and the other major religions of the world will immediately reveal that the common ground between Judaism, Christianity and Islam is not accidental or incidental but essential, fundamental and unique.

The precise place of Judaism within the 'monotheistic family' is an interesting and debatable question. Judaism is often described as the parent of the other two religions, and here we meet the first major ambiguity in the use of the term 'Judaism'. Christianity and Islam are both religions with an obvious beginning in time, even though both recognize that they have an important 'prehistory'. Thus the terms 'pre-Christian' and 'pre-Islamic' both have a recognizable meaning, and both terms are in fact in current use. But Judaism has no obvious starting-point, and the term 'pre-Jewish' is not used. Judaism and Christianity both share a body of ancient sacred scriptures (indeed they constitute one of the most important areas of common ground between the two religions): Jews call them the Bible whereas for Christians they are only part of the Bible—the 'Old Testament'. Judaism has evolved by gradual stages, and Jews, even though they recognize later developments, tend to consider the religion of the Bible as essentially the same religion as the Judaism that has existed ever since. But Christians, while considering the Old Testament as an important source of their religion, tend to see it as a 'pre-Christian', and more particularly as a 'Jewish' document. In Christian usage, therefore, the term 'Judaism' often refers to the biblical 'prehistory' of Christianity, or to the Jewish religion as it existed at the time of Christ. It is in this sense that Judaism is described as the parent-religion of Christianity. And similarly in the case of Islam: as Christianity presents itself as a new revelation superseding the earlier Judaism, so Islam presents itself as a new revelation superseding both Judaism and Christianity.

All this belongs to the mutual polemic between the three religions, and each claim has some historical justification. But it must be emphasized that this way of looking at the relationship between the three religions has little or no bearing on their individual character or mutual relationship today. Perhaps it would be more realistic to view the three as brothers or sisters rather than as parent and children, or as three branches of the same tree rather than two branches deriving from the same Jewish trunk. But all such images are inadequate and they fail to do justice to the complexity of the relationship. In this book we shall be concerned with Judaism as it exists today, and not with the Judaism of Christian polemic, which in any case, it must be said, is a theological abstraction bearing only a tangential relationship with any historical manifestation of the Jewish religion.

Having considered some of the positive merits of the conception of Judaism as one of the monotheistic religions, it is time to consider some of its shortcomings. And it must be admitted that, from a Jewish point of view, they are real and serious. What the objections boil down to is a feeling that Judaism is misrepresented as being essentially the same kind of thing as Christianity or Islam, and a particular source of difficulty here is the concept of a religion. Judaism is often described by Jews as being 'not so much a religion, more a way of life', and what this saying reveals is a deep-seated unease about the definition of Judaism as a religion. This widely felt unease, which may well appear paradoxical at first sight, deserves deeper scrutiny.

The use of the word 'religion' to mean primarily a system of beliefs can be fairly said to be derived from a Christian way of looking at Christianity. The comparative study of religions is an academic discipline which has been developed within Christian theology faculties, and it has a tendency to force widely differing phenomena into a kind of strait-jacket cut to a Christian pattern. The problem is not only that other 'religions' may have little or nothing to say about questions which are of burning importance for Christianity, but that they may not even see themselves as religions in precisely the way in which Christianity sees itself as a religion. At the heart of Christianity, of Christian self-definition, is a creed, a set of statements to which the Christian is required to assent. To be fair, this is not the only way of looking at Christianity, and there is certainly room for, let us say, a historical or sociological approach. But within the history of Christianity itself a crucial emphasis has been placed on belief as a criterion of Christian identity. It has been plausibly argued that the Christian creeds originated as tests of authentic Christian allegiance, and the great divisions within Christendom, whatever may have been their underlying social, cultural or political causes, have tended to be articulated as theological differences. In fact it is fair to say that theology occupies a central role in Christianity which makes it unique among the 'religions' of the world.

It is not necessary here to consider the implications of all this for the study of religions in general, but it is certainly necessary to ponder the implications for the study of Judaism. And in the first place it must be pointed out that the very term 'religion' has been foreign to Judaism until relatively recently, when the dialogue with Christianity has compelled Jews to recognize and use it. Indeed the Hebrew language does not really have a word for 'religion'. In modern Hebrew the word *dat* has been pressed into service to translate 'religion', but it is a word which properly belongs to the realm of law, not belief. A more obvious contender might be the word *emunah*, but *emunah*, which is a key word in the Jewish religious vocabulary, properly means 'trust': belief *in*, rather than belief *that*.

Even the word 'Judaism', it might be added, is a relative new-comer to the Jewish vocabulary in the sense of the religion of the Jews. This word, like so much of the Jewish religious terminology in English (we may think of such words as 'pentateuch', 'prophet', 'phylactery', 'proselyte', even 'Bible' and 'synagogue'), is of Greek origin; it is an abstract noun formed from the word for 'Jew'. In its original use it does not refer to belief but rather means something like 'Jewish identity'. Hebrew for a long time had no equivalent for the usual Christian meaning of 'Judaism'. The abstract noun *Yahadut* meant Jewish identity, the condition of being a Jew, until in modern times it was given the normal meaning of Judaism, which had by now been adopted by Jews speaking English and other western languages.

This history of the word 'Judaism' brings us face to face with a phenomenon which is of the utmost importance in understanding Judaism. To be a Jew means first and foremost to belong to a group, the Jewish people, and the religious beliefs are secondary, in a sense, to this corporate allegiance. The contrast with Christianity is self-evident. The Christian also belongs to a corporate entity, the Christian Church, but the Church is defined as the body of Christian believers, and the Christian is defined in turn by his beliefs. Religious belief is only one ingredient in the makeup of the Jew, and it may not be the most important ingredient at that.

Indeed there are many people in the world who consider themselves to be loyal Jews in every respect and who would deny that they have any religion at all. And, however strange it may appear to the Christian who is used to thinking of religions in theological terms, the role of theology in Judaism has been distinctly secondary, and some leading Jews, both in the past and today, have viewed it with the deepest suspicion. This in itself makes Judaism something very different from Christianity.

If Judaism cannot, without unacceptable sacrifice, be reduced to a system of beliefs, there is another approach to the study of religions which may produce more helpful results. This is the sociological approach which concentrates in the first instance not on statements of belief but on observable phenomena such as worship and ritual. The strength of this approach is that it can be applied to any society, whether or not it considers itself a 'religious' community and even if it does not explicitly articulate its theological ideas. In this way we may study, for example, the 'religion' of the Greeks or Romans, and from observing the phenomena we may argue to the underlying religious beliefs of the society. In the case of Judaism there is abundant material in the form of institutions, public and private worship, ritual observances, and so forth. What is more, this material would be acknowledged by many Jews as being far more central to Judaism than religious beliefs or theological doctrines.

Nevertheless, valuable though the sociological approach can be, it is doubtful whether it can really help us to an understanding of what Judaism is, let alone provide us with a realistic description or analysis of it. There are two main reasons for this. The first is the problem of scale. The sociological approach works best with a small and localized society. If we try to apply it to Jews worldwide, living under very different conditions and for the most part not forming distinct groups but scattered among a non-Jewish majority, we shall first have enormous difficulty in collecting and collating our material, and we may well end up by wondering whether we are studying a single phenomenon or an apparently infinite variety of different 'Judaisms'. It is certainly true, and generally accepted, that Judaism (particularly in terms of observance) takes different forms in different places, or indeed even in the same place; but it is also strongly felt that there is a single thing called 'Judaism', which is not just the lowest common denominator of Jewish observance worldwide.

The second problem, which is perhaps even more intractable, is the difficulty of deciding which phenomena to study. In addition to worship and related activities, which would qualify as 'religious' under any definition, there are many other aspects of Jewish life whose status is more equivocal. For many Jews the food they eat, even the clothes they wear, are an expression of their Jewish identity. How is the observer to select the elements which are relevant to his investigation without producing results which would be, to say the least, bizarre? For some selection, when faced with such a wealth of possible material, is inevitable. The danger is that we may be tempted, once again, to import definitions which derive from Christianity, and to seek out in Judaism the familiar elements of Christian religion, or their close equivalents. This can be misleading. It is tempting, for example, to see the synagogue as the Jewish equivalent of a church, and the rabbi as the equivalent of the Christian priest or minister. Now, it is true that in Christian countries the synagogue has come to resemble a church and the rabbi has assumed many of the functions of a minister of religion. But the traditional roles of the synagogue and the rabbi contain important elements which are not precisely religious in the Christian sense of the word. Conversely, there are institutions in traditional Judaism, such as the bathhouse or the abattoir, which probably deserve to be classified as religious even though they have no obvious Christian equivalent. The non-Jewish student of Judaism, particularly if he is accustomed to thinking in terms of Christianity, must be constantly on his guard against his own preconceptions.

Is Judaism, then, a religion? Or is religion simply one ingredient of Judaism? There is no clear answer to either question; at the very least Judaism challenges conventional ideas of what we mean by a religion. There are Jews today, particularly in Israel, who describe themselves as 'religious' or 'secular' Jews; but the 'secular' Jews do engage in activities which are, on the face of it, religious, while the 'religious' Jews may be hard put to it to define what precisely is religious in their lives, or indeed they may claim that everything they do is religious. In the chapters which follow we shall use the words 'religion' and 'religious' in the way they are normally used by theologians and sociologists, and we shall see that there is a great deal in Judaism which is religious in the usual sense of the word. We must be aware of the theological and sociological dimensions, but we must beware of imposing on Judaism categories which are alien to it. And for that reason our basic approach will be neither theological nor sociological but historical. This is an approach which arises out of Judaism itself and makes use of categories which are familiar in Jewish thought.

A historical approach is not the same thing as a history. This book is not a history of Judaism. Its subject is Judaism as it exists today. But the basic premise underlying the book is that Judaism can only be fully understood historically: that is to say, it is by understanding how Judaism came to be what it is that we can best understand what it is. That is because Judaism must be defined (as its name suggests) in terms of the Jewish people, and a people is defined historically, as a group of people sharing a common history.

This fact is well recognized in one of the few modern attempts at a concise definition of Judaism. It is the definition which opens the Declaration of Principles adopted by the (Reform) Central Conference of American Rabbis at its meeting at Columbus, Ohio, in 1937 (and consequently known as the Columbus Platform): 'Judaism is the historical religious experience of the Jewish people.' Like any short definition, this is only a beginning, and it is in need of further elucidation (particularly of the deliberately vague expression 'historical religious experience'). But it has the great merit of avoiding the pitfalls we have considered above, and pointing instead to the central fact that the character of Judaism is to be sought not in ideas or beliefs but in history. This is not to say that Judaism has no ideas or beliefs, which would be patently untrue, but rather that it is the historical experience which is primary, and the ideas and beliefs in some sense flow from that experience.

The historical approach is able to do justice, as other approaches do not, both to the diversity of Jewish expressions and at the same time to the essential unity of Judaism. The diversity is the outcome of historical experience, and all the different trends and movements, however innovatory, are profoundly conscious of their roots in the Judaism of past generations.

The historical approach is not at odds with a theological or sociological approach, but seeks to complete and enrich them by supplying the crucial insights which they lack. Theologically

1
A People and its Faith

You have chosen us out of all the peoples, loved us and
cherished us. You have raised us up out of all the
nations, set us apart through your commandments, and
drawn us close to you, our King, so as to serve you,
pronouncing over us your great and holy Name.

From the Service for Festivals

A week after their birth male Jewish babies are circumcised; this
is also the occasion on which the child receives his name. Circumcision is a minor surgical operation, involving the removal of the
foreskin, but for Jews it is far more than this: it is a visible symbol
of the covenant between God and the people of Israel. Hence it is
called in Hebrew *brit milah*, 'Covenant of Circumcision', often
shortened simply to *brit*, 'Covenant'.

In the course of the prayers at a circumcision, reference is made
to the covenant of Abraham, who circumcised his son Isaac when
he was a week old, and to the biblical commandment that all male
children should be circumcised. Abraham is called 'our father',
and the image of genealogical descent is prominent in the biblical
wording of the covenant:

I shall make you extremely fruitful and make you into nations; kings
will descend from you. I shall keep my covenant between me and you and
your descendants after you through their generations as a perpetual
covenant, to be God to you and your descendants after you. I shall give
you and your descendants after you the land where you are an alien, the
whole land of Canaan, as a perpetual possession: I shall be God to them.
And God also said to Abraham: You too shall keep my covenant, you
and your descendants after you through their generations.

This covenant, of which circumcision is the symbol, is thus the
enduring bond between God and the descendants of Abraham.
But descent is not to be understood in a genetic sense, as we can
see a little later in the instructions for the Passover offering,
commemorating the Exodus from Egypt under Moses:

The whole community of Israel shall make it. If there is any alien living among you he shall make a Passover offering to the Lord: every male is to be circumcised, and then he can join in making it and be like a native of the land, but no uncircumcised man may eat any of it. The instruction is the same whether for the native or the alien living among you.

The Hebrew word for 'alien', *ger*, is the same word we now use for a proselyte, and male proselytes still undergo the ceremony of circumcision. And like native-born Jews, they receive a Hebrew name on this occasion. But whereas born Jews bear their father's name (for example 'Miriam daughter of Joseph' or 'Jacob son of Reuben'), proselytes have the patronymic 'son/daughter of Abraham our father'. This is a way of reaffirming that they are entering into the covenant of Abraham.

The Passover offering, like other animal sacrifices, is no longer offered by Jews, but the Passover meal is still observed annually as a commemoration of the Exodus; indeed it has remained one of the most popular of all Jewish ceremonies. The dominant theme of Passover is liberation from oppression and bondage, but we are reminded that it was at the Exodus from Egypt that Israel became a people, a process which was sealed at the great assembly at Mount Sinai and brought to fruition in the entry into the promised land after Moses' death. Passover, together with the two other 'pilgrim festivals' of Weeks and Tabernacles, is thus a recurring celebration of the momentous events by which Israel was forged into a people dedicated to the service of the God who made the covenant with Abraham.

The name of this people, Israel, is the name given to Abraham's grandson Jacob on the occasion when he wrestled by night with an unnamed man at the ford of Jabbok. Later tradition interprets this encounter as symbolic of the struggle between the people of Israel and the other nations of the world, which has been such an enduring feature of Jewish history. It is an encounter which ends in a blessing for Israel. In the biblical story, however, Jacob interprets it as an encounter with God, and Jewish commentators have attached great importance to the final element of the name, 'el', which is one of the names of God. It is as if the whole people of Israel bears God's name as its special badge.

Israel is the name by which the people is known in the Bible, and it has remained the name of the people in Hebrew and in other languages wherever the influence of the Bible is strong. The other names in common use in various languages, 'Hebrews' and 'Jews', also go back to the Bible. Abraham is called a Hebrew, and the prophet Jonah, when asked to name his land and people, replied 'I am a Hebrew'; in the Book of Esther, Mordecai is called a Jew. 'Hebrew' has remained important as the name of the language which Jews often call 'the holy tongue', the language of the Bible and the liturgy, as well as of the modern state of Israel. The word 'Jew' is derived from Judah, the ancient territory of which Jerusalem was the capital, and which Jews in ancient times looked to as their homeland. All three names, therefore, are rich in historical and emotional connotations; but Israel is the name to which a special sanctity attaches.

The history of the people of Israel is long and complex: few peoples in the world today have such a long recorded history. To resume it adequately here would be an impossibility; we can only survey some of its main features, so as to provide an essential chronological framework for the chapters which follow. At the risk of oversimplification, the history can be conveniently divided into three periods, ancient, medieval, and modern. Two epoch-making changes in the basic conditions of Jewish life determine this tripartite division: the first is the rise to political hegemony of Christianity and somewhat later of Islam, and the second is the eclipse of that hegemony. Neither of these changes is an event which can be dated to a precise moment, indeed the second, at least so far as Islam is concerned, is not complete even today. But the effect of the changes is clear enough, and they are of fundamental importance for an understanding of Jewish history.

In the first period, which came to an end with the establishment of the political power of Christianity in the fourth and fifth centuries and of Islam in the seventh and eighth centuries, the foundations of Judaism were laid, and its classical literature, the Bible and Talmud, was written. The period can be further subdivided into three parts, which we may call the biblical period, the Greek period, and the Talmudic period.

The biblical period, that is to say the period described in the Bible, encompasses the remote beginnings of the Jewish people as Middle Eastern nomads, the settlement in the Land of Israel and the establishment of the monarchy, the destruction of the northern kingdom of Israel by the Assyrians and of the southern kingdom of Judah by the Babylonians, and the return and rebuilding of Jerusalem under Persian rule. The story is familiar enough to anyone acquainted with the Bible, and the salient features to bear in mind are the building of the Temple in Jerusalem as a focus for Israelite worship and national identity in the tenth century BCE, the sense of desolation on the destruction of that Temple in 587 BCE, the formative crisis of the subsequent Babylonian exile, and the revival of national hope at the time of the Persian restoration and the rebuilding of the Temple. The experience of exile and return was to leave a lasting imprint on the collective Jewish mind, and would help the Jews to weather many another catastrophe in the future with optimism, while giving rise to a complex philosophy of alienation and estrangement. It also caused a dramatic broadening of horizons which affected the conception of God: while still having his home in Jerusalem, he rules over all the nations, and he can even refer to Cyrus, the Persian king, as 'my anointed'.

The Greek period lasts approximately from the conquest of the Persian empire by Alexander the Great of Macedon (331 BCE) until the destruction of the second Temple in 70 CE. This period saw a real widening of the frontiers of the Jewish world: by its end there were Jewish communities throughout the Middle East and the eastern Roman empire and as far to the west as Spain. This dispersion (commonly known still by its Greek name, diaspora) has remained a fact of Jewish life to the present day. The encounter with Greek culture gave rise to traumatic conflicts, but it also produced a notable Greek-Jewish culture which aimed to conserve the best of Greek and Jewish thought. The latter part of the period is marked by a striking variety of more or less radical movements in Judaism, including Pharisaism and nascent Christianity.

In the Talmudic period the Jewish world was divided between the successor-empires of the Greeks, that of the Parthians and later of the Sasanians in the east, and that of the Romans in the west. The Land of Israel (called Palestine by the Romans) was under Roman rule, while the prosperous communities of Babylonia were in the eastern empire. Judaism developed in both centres under the guidance of rabbis, who were the heirs of the priests and scribes of the previous period. The rabbis undertook the codification of Jewish law, which had evolved considerably since biblical times, and embodied their discussions and decisions in the Talmudic literature. They strove to eliminate diversity of belief and practice, and to establish consistent and universal norms. Rabbinic Judaism was to retain its dominance for most Jews throughout the long Middle Ages.

In the ancient period the Jews, scattered as they were, had known moments of oppression and persecution and disastrous wars, but by and large they had enjoyed what can be called normal conditions of life. In many places they had been accorded special privileges, which allowed them to preserve their distinctive customs and lifestyle even when these were at odds with the prevailing laws and culture. A minority virtually everywhere, they had maintained their identity with tenacity and had shown great powers of adaptation. These qualities were to be put severely to the test in the ensuing period, when the basic conditions under which they lived were completely changed. Since the rise of Christianity, Jews and Christians had been involved in an ideological conflict which was also a competition for souls and for power and influence. With the adoption of Christianity as the official religion of the Roman empire in the early fourth century and the consolidation of Christian influence in the fifth century, the opportunities open to the Jews became progressively reduced. Their economic and social life was circumscribed, they were prevented from seeking proselytes, and they were subjected to a system of what is now called apartheid: they were deprived of access to political power and to the educational institutions of the majority culture, their contacts with Christians were limited, and eventually they were forced to live in separate quarters in the cities and even to wear distinctive clothing. They also frequently suffered physical attacks by Christian mobs, and harsh and arbitrary decrees, including expulsion from Christian cities and states. Under these conditions the Jews were thrown back on their own resources, and it is remarkable how well they managed to maintain their existence, their way of life and their culture.

Meanwhile the conquest of the Middle East and north Africa by Muslim Arabs in the seventh century led to similar, if less oppressive, conditions being established here too. Although the discriminatory regulations were often not applied in their full rigour, there was always the risk of a change of policy, and massacres and religious persecutions were not unknown. Despite these hardships there were opportunities for Jews to benefit from, and even contribute to, Islamic culture. In general, however, the Middle Ages must be seen as a period of continuation and consolidation for Judaism rather than of innovation or creativity.

The medieval period, like the ancient period, can be subdivided into three sections. The first is often called the Gaonic period, because of the authority exercised by the Geonim (plural of Gaon), the heads of the main Talmudic academies of the Middle East. They were responsible for elaborating the teachings of the Talmud and spreading them to other parts of the Jewish world. The main achievement of the Geonim was in the field of Jewish law, where their codifications and responsa (replies to specific enquiries) laid the foundations for later work. They also applied themselves to the standardization of the liturgy and of the text of the Hebrew Bible.

The Gaonic period ended in the eleventh century with the decline of the Gaonic academies and a shift of the centre of gravity of the Jewish world westwards, to north Africa and Spain, and to a lesser extent to north-western Europe. The period which followed saw the flowering of Jewish philosophy, Bible commentary, and Hebrew poetry, both sacred and profane. The great names of this period, such as the philosopher Moses Maimonides, the philosopher-poets Solomon Ibn Gabirol and Judah ha-Levi, the commentators Rashi, Abraham Ibn Ezra and David Kimhi and the poets Samuel ha-Nagid, Moses Ibn Ezra and Immanuel of Rome are only the tip of a massive cultural iceberg. This was also the classical period of Jewish mysticism, whose major work, the Zohar, appeared in Spain in the late thirteenth century. The great illuminated Hebrew manuscripts which are among the treasures of medieval Europe are another reminder of the cultural richness of the period.

The expulsion of the Jews from Spain in 1492, coinciding with the completion of the Christian reconquest of the country, marks the end of an era. After a long series of persecutions and expulsions, Spain was the last Christian country where Jews had survived in large numbers. Many of those expelled from Spain found a safe refuge in the Ottoman empire, where centres like

Constantinople and Salonica now rose to prominence. Communities of Spanish Jews were also established in other parts of the Mediterranean basin and eventually in Hamburg, Amsterdam and London and in the New World. The Jews of Spanish origin are known as Sephardim, from Sepharad, the Hebrew name for Spain. The term is used to distinguish them from Ashkenazim, Jews of German origin. The expulsions from France and the central European states had pushed the Ashkenazim eastwards into Poland, where they found a welcome and later participated in the prosperity and cultural flowering of the country in the sixteenth and seventeenth centuries. In time, particularly as a result of the disturbances caused by the Cossack rebellion of 1648, there was a reverse migration westwards, bringing throngs of Yiddish-speaking Ashkenazim back towards the Rhineland where their ancestors had originated. These various upheavals transformed the shape of the Jewish world, and brought about corresponding changes in the character of Jewish culture. On the one hand, there was a tendency to retreat from the 'real world' into esoteric speculation and the pursuit of instant salvation. In the small town of Safed, in the mountains of Galilee, a rich school of mysticism emerged in the sixteenth century and soon extended its influence abroad. In eastern Europe the charismatic revivalism of the Hasidim attracted an enormous following in the late eighteenth century. But there was also a contrary tendency, a broadening of horizons due to the contact with other cultures, and notably with the humanism of the European Renaissance. The spread of printing, accelerated by the movements of population, assisted the diffusion of Jewish culture and gave a stimulus to scholarly activity, with Italy, where Jews shared in the excitement of the Renaissance, setting the lead, closely followed by central Europe and the Ottoman empire. In prosperous Amsterdam, too, where numbers of crypto-Jews whose ancestors were forcibly converted to Christianity in Portugal returned to the faith of their forefathers, there was an astonishing cultural efflorescence. Here, and in a few other western centres, the tide of history was turning, and the first steps were being taken towards the emancipation of the Jews from their condition of segregation and subjection.

The modern age is commonly considered to begin with the French

Revolution in 1789, but it should be remembered that for the Jews the Revolution marked only a beginning. Even in France it was a long time before they achieved full civic equality, and for many important parts of the Jewish world, including all the most populous regions, the process took much longer. Russia, for example, had to wait until the Revolution of March 1917, and even today there are some Arab countries where Jews are barely tolerated or even completely excluded.

The modern period, like the others, can be divided into three parts. The first and longest, from the French Revolution to the Russian Revolution, was the period in which political emancipation was achieved in most European countries. On the religious and intellectual planes, it was a period in which traditional ideas were radically rethought, a period of great creativity and renewed vitality. This was the age of the Haskalah (enlightenment) movement, in which the Jews of Europe were gradually introduced to the new currents of European culture. It was also the age of religious reforms, when the new movements which we now know as Orthodoxy, Reform and Conservative Judaism were evolved through the adaptation of traditional beliefs and practices to modern ways of thought and life. Meanwhile the often painful process of emancipation, and the emergence of a resistance to it in the form of antisemitism, gave rise to other new trends, notably various manifestations of Jewish socialism and nationalism, which were particularly strong in central and eastern Europe. The relative unity of the medieval period was submerged in a turmoil of conflicting factions, reminiscent of the Greek period nineteen centuries earlier. And to cap it all this period saw the greatest mass movement of population that the Jewish world has ever known, caused mainly by economic hardship, and directed mainly to the United States of America. It has been estimated that between 1881 (when outbreaks of violence in Russia gave an added boost to emigration) and 1914 (when the outbreak of the First World War temporarily impeded the movement of population) more than two million Jews—well over a quarter of all the Jews in the world—left Europe. America, with its religious and political freedom and its economic opportunities, was rapidly becoming a major centre of the Jewish world.

The year 1917 was a turning-point for the Jews in several respects. In Russia, the country with the largest Jewish population in the world, the Revolution in March swept away at a stroke all the repressive legislation which made the life of the Jews so abnormal and difficult. It was welcomed with euphoric enthusiasm, and even the Bolshevik seizure of power eight months later was not seen at first as a danger. It led, however, to a ruthless onslaught on religion: the communal structures were abolished, schools and synagogues were closed down, rabbis were arrested and deported, and religious books and ritual objects were confiscated. The practice of the religion was virtually outlawed and driven underground. A different kind of turning-point was the British military advance into Palestine, coupled with the Balfour Declaration, issued on 2 November 1917. The Declaration offered the British Government's support for the establishment of a Jewish National Home in Palestine, and for the first time this aim of the Zionist movement appeared as a realistic possibility and not just a pipe-dream. After a painful struggle it was eventually achieved on 14 May 1948 with the declaration of an independent state of Israel. Also in 1917, the American intervention in the European war was accompanied by an assumption of responsibility by American Jews for the fate of their brethren in Europe. Plans were made to secure civil rights after the war for Jews in those countries which still denied them, and these rights were in fact eventually written into the peace treaties drawn up at Versailles. Henceforth the Jews of America were to play a guiding role in Jewish destiny. The period 1917–48, then, was a period of severe tribulation for the Jews of Russia, a period of rapid progress in the face of persistent difficulties for the Zionist movement, and a period of coming of age and increasing importance on the world Jewish scene for American Jewry. But it was also the period which saw the gradual rise to power in Germany of a political movement committed to the final solution of the so-called 'Jewish' question, and of a nightmare ordeal for the Jews of Europe, more than half of whom were brutally murdered and many of the remainder driven overseas as refugees. The annihilation of six million Jews by the Nazis and their collaborators is a blow from which the Jewish people has not yet recovered, either physically or psychologically; indeed, it is hard to see how a complete recovery is possible. At any rate the horror of the Nazi holocaust will surely continue to haunt the collective Jewish memory for many generations to come.

The period since 1948 is the period of the state of Israel, a haven of refuge for the victims of repression and a vital symbol of national revival and hope for all Jews in the world. It is a period which has seen the emigration of most of the Jews of north Africa and Asia, relatively untouched by the holocaust, and in Europe a painful reconstruction on the rubble of a ruined past. The rise of the United States of America to a position of dominance in the Jewish world is now complete: it accounts for some 44 per cent of the world Jewish population, while Israel has 25 per cent, the USSR 13 per cent, and smaller but still significant numbers exist in France, Great Britain, Canada, Argentina, Brazil, and South Africa.

It is facts such as these that need to be borne in mind when studying Judaism today. It is estimated (reliable statistics being impossible to ascertain in most countries) that there are some 13 or 14 million Jews in the world today, as against estimates of slightly under 17 million in 1939. Ninety-five per cent of them live in the nine countries just named, and it is interesting to note that in all over 50 per cent live in English-speaking countries. Moreover, with the exception of Israel, whose population is predominantly Jewish, Jews everywhere constitute a barely significant minority: even in the USA they are barely 2.5 per cent of the total population. Of course there are, as there always have been, local concentrations: in New York City, for example, the Jews are reckoned to form 16 per cent of the total population. But even this is still a small minority, and New York is thoroughly exceptional. Before the holocaust the picture was different. In eastern Europe, and especially in Poland, there were large concentrations of Jews, and some towns actually had a majority of Jewish inhabitants. Another important change is that the Jews are predominantly an urban population everywhere (again with the exception of Israel), and the tendency to urbanization is still continuing. And yet another fact to bear in mind is that, as a result of the massive movements of population which have taken place in the past hundred years or so, Jews everywhere tend to be immigrants, or the children or grandchildren of immigrants. There are very few places indeed where a majority of the Jews have long-established local roots. All these facts have an important bearing on the outlook and attitudes, and to some extent also on the religious beliefs and practices, of the Jews. They are a small people with a strong sense of their own importance and destiny; a scattered people with a strong sense of unity; an urban people whose religion still bears many traces of a rural past; an ancient people whose roots are generally not in the place where they currently live.

The precise meaning of the word 'people' as applied to the Jews has often given rise to confusions and misconceptions. It is much easier to see what the Jews are not than what they are. They are not a race, in the modern, biological sense of the word: there are no genetic features which all Jews share, and which are peculiar to them; indeed, since it has always been possible for non-Jews to become Jews it could hardly be expected that there should be. They are not a religious community, in the sense that Christians, for example, are: the concept of Jewish unity embraces people who have many different religious beliefs, or none at all. They are not a political entity: Jews live under many different political systems, as loyal citizens of many different states, without feeling that there is any inherent conflict between their Jewish identity and their citizenship. Nor are they merely a national or ethnic minority. All these labels have been used, and none is satisfactory, even though they all contain perhaps a germ of truth. Jews *do* have some of the attributes of ethnic minorities in some countries, they *do* sometimes express their identity in political terms, they *do* often see themselves as a religious group, and they *do* acknowledge a hereditary element in Jewish identity, in that a child of Jewish parents is considered to be a Jew from the moment he or she is born. But none of the labels is sufficient to define Jewish existence.

Are the Jews then something unique? Certain parallels suggest themselves: the Armenians, for example, are a scattered people who retain a strong sense of identity wherever they are, and this identity is passed on from parents to children and is closely tied to a distinctive religion. Similar remarks might apply to other peoples, too, such as the Welsh and the Scots, the Basques or the Irish. All are peoples in a sense which is not quite identical with the modern sense of 'nationality', with an identity which cannot be defined entirely in political terms, and all are acquainted with the phenomenon of diaspora. One detail which makes them rather different from the Jews is that historically they all have a much more continuous record of settlement in a particular place, with which they are especially associated. There have always been Jews in the Land of Israel, but their numbers have been relatively small and, however strong the attachment of Jews everywhere to the Land, the main events of Jewish history, from late antiquity to the early part of this century, have taken place elsewhere. But the parallels are suggestive; they confirm that the key to Jewish identity is to be sought not in any abstract definition but in history. What makes the Jews a people ultimately is the sense of a shared past, a common historic experience which unites people in different parts of the world even if it has not affected them personally or their ancestors.

To be a Jew is thus to acknowledge an attachment to this historic experience. Conversion to Judaism is often conceived in religious terms, but religion is only one aspect of Jewish identity. One cannot become a Jew through subscribing to a set of religious beliefs, any more than one ceases to be a Jew by losing one's religious faith. (We do not speak of 'a lapsed Jew'.) Hence converts are normally spoken of not as converts but as proselytes, a Greek term which originally meant 'immigrants'. To become a Jew is essentially to join a people.

The Jewish historical experience has important consequences for the ways Jews see themselves, and also for their religious beliefs, since these beliefs are formed by historical experience. The Jews have never been a large people. On the contrary, even in the Bible the idea is several times expressed that God chose the people of Israel precisely because they were a small people. It is true that God's promise to Abraham included an undertaking to multiply his descendants 'like the stars in the sky and the sand on the seashore', and this promise seems to have been fulfilled in part during the period of slavery in Egypt, when the Israelites grew from a small clan with seventy members to a large people, numbering 600,000 adult males. But this growth, which is highlighted in the Passover service, has to be set in the context of the whole biblical narrative and the subsequent historical experience, where the people of Israel are seen to be a small and vulnerable people, always at the mercy of greater and more powerful nations.

The survival of this small, scattered, powerless people from remote antiquity to the present day in the face of repeated attacks and persecutions may well appear as little less than miraculous. Since the genocidal onslaught of the Nazi period it has even been suggested that survival should be considered a religious imperative. The theme of survival, however, has been a subject of reflection since at least the time of the Babylonian exile, and the traditional consensus is that it lies in the hand of God, not of man. As the Passover ritual says, reviewing the lessons of the Exodus from Egypt: 'The promise made to our fathers holds good for us also: for not only did one man attack us to annihilate us, but in every single generation people attack us to annihilate us, but the Holy One, blessed be he, rescues us from their power.'

The age-old tension between the universal and the particular in Judaism is a manifestation of the conflicting claims of promise and reality. Jewish universalism looks to the whole world as God's domain: the Jews are chosen by God to convey a message to all mankind. Jewish particularism sees the covenant with Israel as complete in itself; the universal role of God as father and king of all mankind is not denied, but is of little concern for the Jew, whose allotted task is to live up to the demands of the covenant. In practice the two diverging tendencies have coexisted more or less easily, but under stress the tension can make itself felt. The faithful Jew, studying his ancient scriptures, can hardly have failed to feel a certain impatience at seeing the divine promises so obviously frustrated. The rise of Messianic movements, with their expectation of impending redemption, is easily understood against this background.

Closely linked with Messianism is the idea of exile. Dispersion, as we have seen, has been a condition of Jewish life for a very long time; indeed, the origins of the diaspora can be traced back at least as far as the Babylonian exile after the destruction of the first Temple. In the Jewish mind, dispersion and exile have remained closely linked ideas: the usual Hebrew term for 'diaspora', *golah* or *galut*, actually means 'exile'. Diaspora is thus not only dispersal, it means estrangement from the homeland, the Land of Israel, which is also the promised land of the covenant. At one crucial moment the Zionist movement was painfully torn apart by the temptation to aim for the establishment of a Jewish national home in whatever territory might be found, rather than persevere with the apparently unattainable goal of Israel. The majority insisted on the Land of Israel, as the historic and sentimental homeland of the Jewish people. But even the successful restoration of Jewish rule in Israel has not

2
Torah and Tradition

Moses received Torah from Sinai and handed it over to Joshua, Joshua to the Elders, the Elders to the Prophets, and the Prophets handed it over to the members of the Great Assembly. They said three things: Be scrupulous in judgment; Raise up many disciples; Make a fence for the Torah. Simeon the Righteous was one of the survivors of the Great Assembly. He used to say: On three things the world stands: Torah, worship, and charitable deeds . . .

. . . Rabban Yohanan ben Zakkai received from Hillel and Shammai. He used to say: If you have learnt much Torah, do not claim the credit for yourself, because that is what you were made for. Rabban Yohanan ben Zakkai had five disciples: Rabbi Eliezer ben Hyrcanus, Rabbi Joshua ben Hananiah, Rabbi Yose the Priest, Rabbi Simeon ben Nathaniel, and Rabbi Eleazar ben Arakh . . .

Sayings of the Fathers

This celebrated rabbinic text, which can be found printed in many prayer books, presents the authentication of Rabbinic Judaism in terms of an unbroken tradition, stretching right back to the revelation at Sinai. The names of biblical figures are joined to those of legendary, mist-shrouded characters of the Greek period, the age of Scribes and Pharisees, until the line narrows down to a single individual, Rabban Yohanan ben Zakkai, a survivor of the Roman conquest of Jerusalem and the supposed founder of Rabbinic Judaism. And from that point the tradition broadens out again to encompass all the early rabbis.

Judaism is a profoundly traditional religion, in the sense that each generation instinctively looks for guidance to the past, and is reluctant to overthrow received values and patterns of behaviour. It is also a religion in which the idea of tradition has always played a vitally important part. At each moment of challenge or crisis the debate has centred on the role to be ascribed to tradition.

Of course tradition plays a large role in other religions as well, but in Judaism there are two factors which bring it into especial prominence. One is the lack of a credal basis, and the other is the lack of a central religious authority. The Jew confronted with new ideas or changed circumstances instinctively turns for guidance to the established norms of the past, since he has neither a canon of faith nor a human authority that he can turn to.

The doctrine of tradition has consequently been one of the pillars of Judaism down the ages, and one which has been none the less effective for being left undefined or unformulated. Judaism does not favour the precise formulation of doctrines, and this can be seen as a source of strength rather than weakness. The lack of definition permits a flexibility, a creative dynamism, which is far more difficult to attain where inherited formulations hamper the process of adaptation to changing needs.

The essential idea of tradition is passing something on (this is the root meaning of the Hebrew word *masoret*. Another way of looking at the same process is in terms of reception, received tradition, and for this Hebrew, unlike many other languages, has a special word, *kabbalah*). Tradition is not only a process, it can also be a thing: a teaching or body of teachings, whether written or unwritten, handed down from generation to generation and considered to be in some sense normative. The content of Jewish tradition at its broadest is very broad indeed, and comprises laws and statements believed to have been revealed by God in words, together with interpretations of these revealed words and commentaries on them; myths, legends and historical narratives; ethical and metaphysical teachings; forms of worship; and practices and observances amounting to a whole way of life.

The word which is most commonly used to refer to the content of Jewish religious tradition is 'Torah'. The basic meaning of 'Torah' is 'instruction' or 'teaching', and it is usually used in the specific sense of authoritative or divine teaching. This reflects the use of the word in the Bible and the liturgy, where Torah is often called 'the Torah of the Lord'. But 'Torah' is actually a word with a very wide range of meanings. At its narrowest, it is the technical term for the most authoritative of the sacred scriptures, the 'Five Books of Moses' or Pentateuch. This is the sense in which it is used in the phrase 'As it is written in the Torah . . .', which occurs frequently in the liturgy. The parchment scroll containing the Five Books which is read in the synagogue is called *Sefer Torah* or 'Book of the Torah'. At its widest, the word 'Torah' embraces the totality of Jewish religious teaching, and a good deal more besides. As one old dictum has it, 'Even the everyday conversation of the learned is Torah and needs to be studied.' And in between these two extremes there is a wide range of other meanings. It can refer to the whole Hebrew Bible, for example. It can mean study, or a particular subject of study, or teaching, or a particular body of teachings.

'Torah' and 'tradition' can be used in practice to refer to the same body of teachings; but there is an important difference of nuance between the two words. When the word 'Torah' is used, the dominant idea is that of revelation: the teachings in question have a claim to authority which is based on their having been revealed by God. When the word 'tradition' is used, the dominant idea is that of continuity: the teachings in question owe their authority to their having been handed down and accepted from generation to generation. These two ideas are not inherently in conflict: I may believe or do something because my forebears believed or did it *and* because I consider that it derives from a divine revelation. But in any particular instance I may consider that it is a human tradition which does not derive directly from divine revelation, or I may consider that what is important is that it is divinely revealed, regardless of its traditional status. This is not merely an academic distinction. The status of revelation and tradition, their authority and rival claims, have often given rise to disagreement. In fact a continuing debate about these very questions has been at the heart of Jewish theological reflection and controversy since ancient times, and the debate still continues today.

One of the most celebrated divisions among Jews in ancient times, that between the Pharisees and the Sadducees, was apparently concerned almost exclusively with the question of the nature and authority of tradition. The Pharisees maintained and revered certain rules of conduct not recorded in the Mosaic laws; they called them 'tradition of the fathers' or 'tradition of the elders'. These traditional teachings brought them into conflict with other groups, and notably with the Sadducees, who taught that only the written laws were to be considered authoritative, and that those from the 'tradition of the fathers' need not be observed. From this time on the word 'tradition' enters Jewish theological discourse, and becomes something of a touchstone of belief and practice.

The rabbis of the Talmudic period, who inherited many of the beliefs of the Pharisees, made tradition a very important part of their theology, although the theory of tradition is nowhere very elaborately worked out. Central to all rabbinic theology is the concept of the revelation at Sinai. What was revealed at Sinai was not only the Torah (in the sense of the Five Books of Moses), but a great deal of other teaching besides, which was handed down by oral tradition. According to one late commentary, God revealed to Moses the whole Bible, the Talmud, the Midrash, and even the answers which would be given at any future time to the questions of a serious student. The accuracy of the traditional teachings is also guaranteed by a faithful chain of transmission going back to Sinai. The rabbis themselves placed great emphasis on the careful transmission of teachings from master to pupil, and they also prized oral tradition at least as highly as written tradition, if not somewhat above it. Written law, oral tradition, long-established custom, rational argument, and even decisions taken by majority vote are all elements in a complex of formulae and equations, which collectively were labelled as Torah and derived from the revelation at Sinai. And the rabbis themselves became the custodians of this rich and ever-growing tradition.

In the Gaonic period a number of dissenting Jewish religious movements arose in the east, in Iraq and Persia, of which Karaism was the most successful. This was a time when the oral traditions of the rabbis had been codified and reduced to writing in the Talmud and other compendious works, and when the political triumph of Islam had facilitated the spread of Rabbinic Judaism from Iraq throughout the Jewish world. The Karaite challenge was directed specifically against the rabbinic doctrine of tradition and the authority of the Talmud. Karaism demanded a return to the authority of the Bible, interpreted where necessary according to the independent judgement of the individual reader, and dependence on the Talmud and the rabbinic tradition of biblical interpretation was decried or ridiculed. With the passage of time, however, a strong attachment evolved to distinctive Karaite traditions, and indeed there was a large measure of acceptance even of rabbinic traditions, provided they did not conflict with scripture. There were even attempts to compile a Karaite 'chain of tradition' going back to Moses, to rival the rabbinic chain of tradition. More important than tradition, however, in Karaite thought was the common consent of the community. This consent or agreement, known in Arabic as *ijma*, plays an important part in Islam, too, and in fact in the early development of Islam there are also tensions between *ijma* and tradition which can be closely paralleled in Jewish thought.

The influence of Islam is particularly noticeable in the area of religious philosophy. After a promising early initiative in the period of Greek dominance, philosophical thought had suffered an eclipse among the Jews, and was not revived until the tenth century, when some Jewish thinkers, following in the footsteps of their Muslim counterparts, began to press reason into the service of religion. It is now that the first systematic expositions of Jewish beliefs were compiled. In the process, the doctrine of tradition had to be refined and clarified. The first of these systematic expositions was the *Beliefs and Opinions* of the Gaon Saadya (882–942), the head of the rabbinic academy of Sura in Iraq. In common with the Muslim thinkers of his time, Saadya's primary concern is with the relationship between reason and revelation, but in the course of his exposition he is obliged to discuss the role of tradition. How do we know anything? All philosophers would agree that knowledge may come through observation or sense-perception, through intuitive judgements, or through logical inference, or indeed through any combination of these. But, Saadya argues, for Jews, as well as for Muslims and Christians, there is a fourth source of knowledge, which is *authentic tradition*. What he has in mind here is very largely the revelation embodied in scripture, together with the traditional interpretation of the sacred text. But he places tradition in a wider context when he argues that without reliance on tradition many accepted aspects of human life would be impossible. Trade, for instance, depends on the acceptance of reports whose truth cannot be guaranteed by personal experience or logic. Law and order depend on our believing that regulations derive ultimately from the ruler, even if we have no other means of checking this. And without tradition no one would be able to identify the property of his parents or grandparents; in fact he could not even be certain who his parents were. 'In consequence, human affairs would always be subject to doubt,' he concludes.

The work of Saadya marks an important step forward, in that the theory of tradition is justified rationally, and is assimilated to a general theory of the reliability of tradition and its dangers. Tradition, for Saadya, is one of the three pillars of Judaism, together with revelation and reason. The relationship between these three pillars is a complex one. Revelation, in the form of scripture, must be interpreted in the light of subsequent tradition. Reason is an invaluable tool, which must be applied to the understanding both of scripture and of tradition, and can be used to resolve any apparent conflict between the two. But reason can never be used to justify the rejection of the explicit teaching of scripture or tradition, even though it may point to the necessity for a figurative interpretation. Thus, although Saadya is at pains to insist on the authority both of reason and of scripture, he allots what amounts to an overriding importance to tradition.

Saadya's *Beliefs and Opinions* can be seen as the starting-point of all subsequent Jewish religious philosophy. Many of his ideas were accepted without question, and the basic problem of the relationship between revelation and reason, and by implication tradition as well, had to be discussed by every philosopher in turn. Naturally different emphases emerged, but the underlying ground of the debate remained the same, and the specific claims advanced on behalf of the trustworthiness of tradition hardly changed for centuries. The Middle Ages as a whole were dominated by an attitude of extreme reverence towards antiquity, which impeded any effort towards new development and independent exploration in religion as much as in science. It is hardly surprising that Jewish thinkers shared in this intellectual outlook. Those thinkers who admitted that progress was possible, and that for example later authorities were sometimes better informed than earlier ones, tended to employ the simile of a dwarf sitting on the shoulders of a giant: the dwarf can see further than the giant, but only because he has the giant underneath him.

This attitude persisted long after a belief in progress had begun to oust the reverence for an ancient golden age in the surrounding European intellectual culture. It was only a small minority of Jewish thinkers at first who dared to take up the new ideas about progress and apply them to Judaism. A leading member of this minority was Abraham Geiger (1810–74), who can be seen as one of the principal founders of Reform Judaism. In a letter written when he was twenty he complained that 'Most rabbis apply all the authority vested in them to the indiscriminate preservation of whatever has been handed down to them by tradition.' The result, he felt, was religious stagnation. Not that Geiger saw himself as an enemy of tradition. On the contrary, he describes tradition in lyrical, almost mystical terms in his book *Judaism and Its History*:

Tradition is the developing power which continues in Judaism as an invisible agent, as a certain ennobling essence that never obtains its full expression, but ever continues to work, transform and create. Tradition is the animating soul in Judaism, it is the daughter of revelation and of equal rank with it . . . Tradition, like revelation, is a spiritual energy that ever continues to work, a higher power that does not proceed from man, but is an emanation from the Divine Spirit, a power that works in the community, chooses its own ministers, manifests itself by its ever purer and riper fruits, and thus preserves vitality and existence itself.

This enthusiastic encomium of tradition is, of course, tendentious. It has to be read against its background, which is the debate between modernists and traditionalists. For the traditionalists, revelation meant the once-for-all revelation at Sinai, enshrined in the written Torah, and tradition meant the oral Torah, embodied in the Talmud and other rabbinic compilations. The traditionalist position is forcefully expressed by one of its leading exponents, Solomon Eiger, in these terms:

The only person who can be considered a conforming Jew is one who believes that the divine law-book, the Torah, together with all the interpretations and explanations found in the Talmud, was given by God himself to Moses on Mount Sinai to be delivered to the Jews and to be observed by them for ever. Moses delivered the oral and the written law which had been revealed to him to his successor Joshua, Joshua to the so-called *zekenim* (elders), these to the prophets, and the prophets to the members of the Great Assembly. These oral divine traditions are the very same ones which are collected in the Talmud and which we are commanded to obey.

For Geiger and other modernist rabbis, neither revelation nor tradition was something fixed once for all time. The Bible, the Talmud, the various commentaries and lawcodes, all were links in a centuries-old chain, but they do not contain the whole of revelation and tradition, and not everything within them is essential and binding. Judaism has become what it is gradually, they argued, and has always been subject to change and development. In the process of change some older elements become obsolete, and if they are wilfully retained they constitute an obstacle to true religiosity.

The battleground in the nineteenth century was at first the Talmud, but it was not long before the biblical tradition was also questioned, in keeping with trends in Christian scholarship. In due course the whole of the Jewish tradition was subjected to scrutiny, and beliefs and practices alike were extensively revised in the interest of making Judaism more attractive to Jews and better adapted to modern ways of life and thought. The conflict between modernists and traditionalists, however, continued unabated, and in between the two extremes a whole gamut of standpoints emerged. Throughout the debates and polemics the concept of tradition was continually evoked by all parties to support their views. The word tradition was used in many different senses, always with positive connotations. The modernists often insisted that they were reviving older elements in the tradition which had become overlooked, and in due course even the more radical reformers developed their own traditions to which they became deeply attached.

Contemporary Judaism is thus deeply marked by the concept of tradition, and at the same time deeply divided over the question of what constitutes authentic tradition, as well as by the question of the authority to be ascribed to tradition. The main trends in contemporary Judaism may be crudely classified under three headings: traditional, modernist, and secular.

Traditionalism (which is sometimes called, misleadingly, 'ultra-Orthodoxy') is characterized by the attempt to exclude new external influences on Judaism, and to preserve, so far as possible, the values and practices which prevailed in the late medieval period. The emphasis is on practice, and on the study of the Talmud and the great legal codes such as the *Shulhan Arukh*. The importance of tradition is not so much that it confers any particular authority in itself, but rather that it guarantees the authentic transmission of the divine revelation. Traditionalists commonly describe themselves as 'Torah-true', meaning that they are the true custodians of the divinely-given commandments.

Traditionalism tends to be deeply suspicious of any knowledge or belief explicitly originating outside the tradition, and this suspicion may extend to long-established elements such as medieval Jewish philosophy. Needless to add, modern philosophical and political ideas are particularly suspect.

Among the modernist movements the most conservative is Orthodoxy. Orthodoxy attempts to combine traditional Judaism with modern western ideas and lifestyle, but never at the cost of sacrificing what is truly important in the former. The object is not to reform traditional Judaism, but rather to make it articulate and attractive to modern Jews. Although many of the outward trappings of medieval Jewish life have been tacitly abandoned, Orthodoxy is meticulous about the maintenance of what are considered to be essential traditional religious observances, and their adaptation, where appropriate, to the conditions of modern life. Unlike traditionalism (with which it has kept close links), Orthodoxy does not demand of its adherents that they should turn their backs on the modern world, but rather that they should uphold the teachings of traditional Judaism in changed conditions, and at the same time apply to Judaism whatever beneficial lessons may be learned from the scientific and technical progress of the modern age. Orthodoxy tends to take a broader view of Jewish tradition than does traditionalism; in keeping with its own important scholarly and rationalist tradition, it tends to play down the elements which may be considered mystical, pietistic or superstitious, and to play up the scholastic and philosophical elements.

At the other extreme of modernism is Reform Judaism (also known as Liberal or Progressive Judaism), which strives, as its name suggests, to reform Judaism so as to bring it in line with modern ways of thought and life. Jewish tradition is one of several sources which are drawn on in achieving this reform, in fact in many ways it is the principal source of Reform beliefs and practices, but it enjoys little or no real authority. As the 'Columbus Platform' of 1937 puts it:

Reform Judaism recognizes the principles of progressive development in religion and consciously applies the principle to spiritual as well as to cultural and social life. Judaism welcomes all truth, whether written in the pages of scripture or deciphered from the records of nature. The new discoveries of science, while replacing the older scientific views underlying our sacred literature, do not conflict with the essential spirit of religion as manifested in the consecration of man's will, heart and mind to the service of God and humanity.

The historical perception of progress in human knowledge is linked to an idea of progressive revelation:

Revelation is a continuous process, confined to no one group and to no one age. Yet the people of Israel, through its prophets and sages, achieved unique insight in the realm of religious truth. The Torah, both written and oral, enshrines Israel's ever-growing consciousness of God and of the moral law. It preserves the historical precedents, sanctions and norms of Jewish life, and seeks to mould it in the patterns of goodness and holiness. Being products of historical processes, certain of its laws have lost their binding force with the passing of the conditions which called them forth. But as a depository of permanent spiritual ideals, the Torah remains the dynamic source of the life of Israel. Each age has the obligation to adapt the teachings of the Torah to its basic needs in consonance with the genius of Judaism.

Conservative Judaism (which is an American development with roots both in Orthodoxy and in nineteenth-century Reform Judaism) combines the ideals of Orthodoxy and Reform by accepting the principle of progress while giving full weight to the claims of tradition. It thus answers to a widely felt need for a middle way between the extremes of Orthodoxy and Reform. When the American Conservative movement was founded in 1913, it declared itself to be 'a union of congregations for the promotion of traditional Judaism'; the implication is that it is more committed to tradition than the Reform movement, while in relation to Orthodoxy it looks to tradition rather than dogma in confronting contemporary problems. Conservatism has been no more successful than the other movements in actually formulating a doctrine of tradition, and in practice it often finds itself reacting against the other two movements rather than striking out on a path of its own.

If the differences between the three main modernist trends appear hard to grasp in theory, they may be better displayed by a concrete example. One very visible difference is in the role allotted to women in public worship. In traditional Rabbinic Judaism women were not allowed to participate in the worship of the synagogue except as spectators, and even this role was severely restricted: women were seated separately from men, often concealed behind a screen or curtain, and sometimes secluded in a separate prayer hall of their own. This segregation is maintained in traditionalist synagogues, and also in Orthodox ones, although here the physical barrier (known as a *mehitsah*) has been reduced to a minimum or even removed altogether. In Orthodox synagogues women may not be counted in the *minyan*, the quorum of ten required for public worship, nor are they called up to the reading of the Torah or permitted to lead the congregation in prayer. In Reform Judaism, on the other hand, all formal differences between the sexes have been abolished. Men and women sit together in the synagogue, and women may perform all functions which may be performed by men, including officiating as rabbis. Conservative synagogues, which are all autonomous, display a great deal of variety between these two extremes, but on the whole they tend to allow more rather than less scope to women. The question of ordaining women rabbis was hotly debated throughout the 1960s and '70s, and eventually it was decided that women could become rabbis. It is interesting that the arguments in this debate tended to centre on traditional Jewish law. What was being sought was apparently an accommodation with the demands of modern life which would not be flagrantly at odds with tradition as explicitly formulated in the legal codes. This quest for compromise between tradition and modernity may be seen as characteristic of Conservative Judaism, which is inherently pragmatic, and strives to avoid the dogmatism of the more extreme movements.

'Secular Judaism' is the name given to the modern phenomenon of Jews who identify with Judaism but reject its religious dimension. This tendency, whose roots are in nineteenth-century Russia, has become an established feature of contemporary Jewry. Unlike the other trends we have discussed, it has developed no coherent ideology, and has no specific institutional base (although it commonly finds expression in various kinds of cultural and political associations). It is therefore rather hard to describe or discuss in the abstract. It does appear though that many people who describe themselves as secular Jews often have a strong attachment to traditional features of Judaism, including what are normally considered to be religious rituals (emptied, of course, of their religious meaning). An obvious example of this is the observance in the non-religious kibbutzim in Israel of the

Sabbath and Jewish festivals, which are given a naturalistic
interpretation that manages to preserve a good deal of their traditional character.

If contemporary Judaism, in all its manifestations, is deeply
marked by the concept of tradition, one reason may be a sense of
loss. The Nazi holocaust, which destroyed the old centres of
traditional life in eastern Europe and exiled European Jews to
unfamiliar surroundings in new lands, is only partly responsible
for this almost palpable feeling of a dramatic break with the past.
The feeling can be traced back to the great migrations of the end
of the last century and beyond, to the social and cultural changes
which had already transformed Jewish life and thought in western
Europe. It is related of Hermann Cohen (1842–1918), the German
philosopher who founded the Marburg school of neo-Kantianism,
that towards the end of his life he showed a visitor a bookcase in
his home full of the old classics of Rabbinic Judaism, and said
with tears in his eyes, 'The *sforim* of my father.' It is impossible
to do justice in English to the poignancy of the Yiddish word
sforim in the mouth of the aged German sage. Literally the word
means simply 'books', but it somehow manages to evoke a whole
lost world. Precisely the same forlorn nostalgia is embodied in
the poem by H. N. Bialik (1873–1934), regarded by Zionists as
the great national poet of the Jewish people, which is entitled
'Before the Bookcase' (and here again the word *sforim* is used):

> Receive my greetings, o ye ancient tomes,
> Accept my kisses, sleepers in the dust.
> From roaming alien isles my soul returns
> And like a homing dove, trembling and tired,
> Stands at the threshold of its childhood nest.
> Do you still recognise your long-lost son
> Who clung, forswearing life, to you alone?
> Of all the pleasures in God's spacious world
> My youthful soul had eyes for you alone:
> My garden in the heat of summer days,
> A pillow for my head on winter nights.
> I pledged within your pages all my mind,
> And in your columns wove my holy dreams.
> Do you remember me? . . .

One effect of the modern combination of pluralism of expression with attachment to tradition has been to highlight the

diversity of the Jewish tradition itself. Each stream of Judaism has tended to seize on elements within the tradition that it finds particularly attractive and important, while rejecting others or consigning them to a secondary status. Jewish tradition now appears less as a single, homogeneous whole than as a complex of interwoven strands. In what follows we shall attempt to unravel some of these strands and study them separately: it must be borne in mind, however, that in reality the various traditions are mutually dependent and have always influenced and nourished each other.

3
The Tradition of Worship

It is therefore our duty to thank you, to praise you, to
glorify you, to bless and sanctify and offer praise and
thanksgiving to your name. Happy are we! How good is
our lot! How pleasant is our destiny! How beautiful our
heritage! Happy are we who, early and late, evening and
morning, twice each day declare:

HEAR O ISRAEL, THE LORD IS OUR GOD, THE LORD IS ONE!

From the morning service

Worship is called in Hebrew *avodah*, which means 'service'. The
underlying idea here is 'service of the Creator', which includes
the whole range of what might be called religious activities, such
as the study of Torah, the observance of the commandments, and
leading an ethical life. Among these various religious activities
worship occupies a special place, and the ancient rabbis refer to it
as 'the service of the heart'. Like the other forms of service, it is
not merely the fulfilment of an obligation, but expresses an attitude of gratitude, devotion, and loyalty. It is a service which is
offered gladly and willingly, and which brings a sense of fulfilment and joy.

The concept of service of the Creator may imply that true
worship consists exclusively of adoration and thanksgiving. It is
true that these have always played an important part in Jewish
worship; but already in the Bible we can find many prayers for
help and favour, side by side with hymns of praise and psalms of
thanksgiving, and these petitionary prayers can be seen as
answering to a deep human need. The rabbis insisted that one
should pray for one's needs, and Jewish worship actually consists
of a mixture of praise and petition, together with penitential
dirges and many other forms of devotion, all expressing in different ways the multifarious bonds which bind man to God.

The concept of service may also suggest a certain tension
between obligation and sincerity: if prayer is obligatory, how can
it be sincere, particularly if the obligation is defined in terms of

the time, form, content of prayers, and even the accompanying gestures? On the one hand, it is easy for such prayer to degenerate into empty formalism; on the other hand where is there room in such a system for joy and sincere emotion? The rabbis debated these problems, and some of them warned against making prayer into a fixed task. But in the course of time the prayers did become fixed, both in their content and wording and also in their external features such as time, place and posture. The problem is far from being resolved, however. The rabbis taught that prayer, like other religious obligations, should be accompanied by *kavvanah*, 'intention', which they understood as 'directing one's mind' to the purpose of one's actions and words. The 'pious men of old' are said to have meditated for an hour, prayed for an hour, and then meditated for a further hour afterwards. *Kavvanah* can be seen as an antidote to the danger of mechanical prayer. Prayer without *kavvanah* was likened by one medieval writer, Bahya Ibn Pakuda, to a body without a soul, and the Baal Shem Tov, the founder of Hasidism, taught that one should say to oneself before beginning to pray that one would be ready to die through powerful concentration during the prayers.

A related problem is the question of public and private prayer. Personal devotion and spontaneity are obviously much harder to achieve during public prayers, and yet a religious community naturally feels a need to express its corporate identity through public worship. Jewish worship today is perhaps primarily associated with the synagogue, although it should be stressed that it is not essential to pray in a congregation, and also that congregational worship can take place virtually anywhere, not just in a building dedicated to the purpose. The synagogue was originally a meeting house probably used primarily for study and instruction. Where and when it became the typical *locus* for Jewish worship is unknown. It has been plausibly suggested that this happened after the destruction of the Temple in Jerusalem, although it would be unrealistic to imagine that once the Temple was destroyed the synagogue immediately replaced it as the focus for public worship. The Temple, with its sacrificial worship administered by hereditary priests, and the synagogue, with its emphasis on the study and exposition of Torah, are really very different kinds of institution. Probably the evolution of the synagogue into a house of prayer had begun long before the Temple was destroyed (many Jews, after all, already lived beyond convenient reach of Jerusalem), and the process was accelerated, particularly within Judaea, in the following generations. The original function of the synagogue as a place of study and teaching is still evident in its furnishing, which consists essentially of a kind of bookcase (known as the holy ark, *aron hakodesh*), which contains the Torah scrolls, and a reading desk. And the reading of the Torah occupies the central place in the major services of the synagogue. The 'perpetual lamp' which burns in front of the ark and the curtain which hangs before the ark in Ashkenazi synagogues recall the biblical sanctuary, but it is interesting that in general there is a conscious avoidance of too overt allusions to the Temple in the furnishing and decoration of the synagogue. (The altar, together with incense and priestly ministers, which became such a prominent feature of the Christian church, is completely absent from the synagogue.)

It also needs to be stressed that, side by side with the synagogue, the home is also an important place of Jewish worship, which is particularly centred cn the table, where the family celebrates the Sabbaths and festivals with time-honoured rituals. Here, if anywhere, is the continuing symbolism of the sanctuary and the altar to be found. The important moments in the life of a Jew are traditionally celebrated in the home rather than the synagogue: these include circumcision and marriage, and the feasting associated with these happy events is a quasi-religious obligation, accompanied with its own blessings. After a death the mourners sit at home on low stools for a week, and members of the community gather to console them and to recite the regular prayers and to offer special prayers for the soul of the departed.

In many cities of the world today there are grandiose synagogue buildings in which worship is conducted in an appropriately solemn and formalized manner. Many of these synagogues were built in the latter half of the nineteenth century or the early part of the present century, at a time of growing prosperity and self-confidence, but they stand in a venerable tradition. They synagogue of ancient Alexandria was described in its day as one of the marvels of the world: it was so large that many worshippers could not hear the leader recite the blessings, and an assistant had to wave a flag to show them when to respond 'Amen'. Excavations have brought to light impressive remains of magnificent ancient synagogues, and there are also some very striking medieval synagogue buildings still surviving, notably in Spain, Italy and Poland. But it has to be said that many older synagogues were more modest affairs, and that Judaism has a very strong 'low church' tradition, characterized by intimacy and informality; it is still alive today, most visibly in the *shtibl*, the small prayer-room once so typical of the popular Judaism of eastern Europe.

The rhythm of Jewish worship, whether in the synagogue or the home, is marked by a strong sense of the passage of time. The basic unit is the day, which is considered to begin in the evening. Prayers are offered regularly in the evening, the morning, and the afternoon, and they are varied to suit the time of day. The central core of the service is the sequence of blessings called *Tefillah* ('the Prayer') by the rabbis and nowadays commonly known as *Amidah* ('standing', because it is recited standing up). In the evening and the morning the *Shema* is also recited: this group of three passages from the Torah begins with the words 'Hear O Israel, the Lord is our God, the Lord is One', which have come to be regarded as a basic affirmation of Jewish faith. Generations of Jews have striven to die with these words on their lips, and two of the three passages are copied on the *mezuzah*, the small parchment scroll which is fixed, usually in an ornamental case, to the doorposts of Jewish homes: they also figure among the passages of Torah which are contained in the *tefillin* or phylacteries, little boxes which are worn during the weekday morning service on the forehead and on the upper arm, next to the heart.

The week leads up to the Sabbath, a sacred day of rest which has its own special prayers. In the synagogue it is marked especially by a reading from the Torah scroll, followed by a passage from the prophets, at the morning service, and by an additional service which follows. Shorter readings from the Torah scroll occur on Sabbath afternoons, and also on Monday and Thursday mornings. In the home there are rituals of welcome for the Sabbath, and there is a custom of singing hymns at the table. The grace before and after meals takes a special form on the Sabbath, as it does also on the various festivals. The sacred character of the Sabbath day demands that it be formally separated from the days that precede and follow: it is inaugurated by the lighting of candles or oil lamps, and its departure is marked by a ceremony known as *havdalah* ('distinction'), involving candle-flames, wine, and fragrant spices.

The month is a lunar month of twenty-nine or thirty days. Ideally the long and short months alternate, but occasional adjustments are made to prevent certain festivals from falling on particular days of the week. In biblical times the day of the new moon was a festival; today it is marked only by some minor variations in the liturgy, and by a public announcement on the preceding Sabbath.

The year is made up of twelve or thirteen months, the additional month being inserted every two or three years, according to a regular cycle instituted in the fourth century CE. This adjustment ensures that Passover always falls in the spring. The passage of the seasons is marked in the regular prayers by subtle variations, but in a larger sense the rhythm of the year as a whole is set by the cycle of the major festivals. The year has two focal points, one in the autumn and the other in the summer, corresponding to the ancient harvest festivals which were celebrated in the Temple period by pilgrimage to Jerusalem. The week-long autumn festival of Tabernacles (*Sukkot*) is preceded by the solemn Days of Awe, framed by the New Year (*Rosh Hashanah*) and the major fast of the Day of Atonement (*Yom Kippur*). Together these constitute a festive period lasting just over three weeks; a month of penitential prayers leads up to it, and it ends with an explosion of joy at *Simhat Torah*, marking the end of the annual cycle of Torah readings. The summer festivals are the week of Passover (*Pesah*) and the feast of Pentecost or Weeks (*Shavuot*). The seven intervening weeks, known as the 'Counting of the *Omer*', were probably a period of joyful celebration in ancient times, but they have come to be marked by a mood of muted sadness. Outside these two periods of major celebrations there are some lesser observances, such as the eight days of *Hanukkah* in midwinter or *Purim* in the early spring.

The forms of Jewish worship as it is practised today have undergone a very long process of evolution, beginning in remote antiquity. Formal worship in the Bible is concentrated on the sacrificial cult of the Temple, and after the final destruction of the Temple this whole elaborate ritual structure came to an end. Nevertheless, the public worship of the biblical period has left many traces in the worship of the synagogue, and not just in the reading of the Torah, which was instituted in biblical times. The Psalms, some of which were originally composed in connection with the Temple services, still feature prominently in Jewish worship today, and other biblical prayers have been incorporated in the liturgy. Moreover, the *Shema*, as we have seen, consists of biblical passages, and according to the rabbis its recitation formed part of the Temple service. Althought the sacrifices themselves have ceased, the biblical regulations of many of the sacrifices are still read in the traditional synagogue service, either within the prayers or as special Torah readings for festive days, while the *Amidah* which is recited in the morning and the afternoon, as well as the additional *Amidah* on Sabbaths and festivals, are thought of as corresponding to the equivalent regular Temple offerings. The most dramatic intrusion of the Temple ritual into that of the synagogue is the *Avodah*, 'the [High Priest's] Service': this is a solemn re-enactment of the ceremonies of the Day of Atonement, the holiest day of the Temple year, which has been inserted into the additional service for that day in the synagogue.

It was the rabbis who standardized the form of the weekday *Amidah* itself, with its nineteen blessings. (Originally they were divided up differently, to give a total of eighteen; in fact the prayer is still often referred to as the 'Eighteen'.) There are many discussions in the rabbinic literature about the precise details of these blessings, and the times and manner of saying them. The literature preserves many private prayers of the rabbis, some of which have also been incorporated in the liturgy, and the rabbis also fixed the form of the grace after meals and of the blessings which are to be recited on various other occasions. The regular prayers thus embody to a high degree the rabbinic beliefs about the nature of God, his relation with the world, and the obligations and aspirations of the Jew. Through being incorporated in the liturgy, these ideas exercised a powerful formative influence on the beliefs of successive generations of Jews, both in the Middle Ages and down to modern times.

The actual process of codification of the liturgy is veiled in obscurity, however, and the oldest complete prayer books date from the Gaonic period. The earliest is traditionally ascribed to the Gaon Amram in the ninth century, and in the following century Saadya produced another important compilation. Meanwhile the prayers began to be adorned with Hebrew liturgical poems (*piyyutim*), which continued to be composed throughout the Middle Ages. In the course of the Middle Ages various liturgical rites developed. Because of the antiquity of the basic prayers, it was in the matter of the *piyyutim* that they tended to differ. Two main streams of development can be discerned, one originating in Palestinian usage, the other deriving from Babylon. The former gave rise to the various rites of Christian Europe, and notably to the Ashkenazi rite, while the latter spread across north Africa to Muslim Spain, and developed into the Sephardi rite, which, with the expulsion from Spain in 1492, was carried back into the Middle East and to other parts of the world. In the Middle Ages there was a proliferation of local rites, but the invention of printing led to the standardization of prayer books and the elimination of many of these.

In the sixteenth century the Kabbalistic centre at Safed which is particularly associated with the name of Isaac Luria, the 'Holy Lion' (1534–72), enriched the liturgy with hymns and meditations of a mystical character, and the 'Rite of the Lion' (*Nusah Ari*) was adopted wherever the Lurianic Kabbalah was influential. In this way a basically Sephardi liturgy came to be used even in Ashkenazi lands, and notably among the Hasidim, who are still attached to it. The Kabbalists and Hasidim placed great emphasis on prayer, particularly on personal, contemplative, and even ecstatic prayer, which was an important vehicle in the individual's quest for communion with God. The Hasidim reacted strongly against the tendency to see prayer as an obligation to be discharged almost mechanically at fixed times. They encouraged the worshipper to put his whole body and soul into his prayer. They stressed music and dancing, and they borrowed tunes freely from external sources. They also disregarded the canonical hours for prayer: as one teacher put it, 'People have souls, not clocks!' Their innovations were strenuously condemned at the time, but in a less intense form they have come to be widely influential.

Reform of Jewish worship bulked large in the modernist movements of the nineteenth century, and the religious conflicts of the period tended to focus particularly on this issue. As a matter of fact, the roots of the movement for liturgical reform can be traced back to the Italian Renaissance. The length of the synagogue services, swollen by innumerable *piyyutim*, the oriental flavour of the traditional chants, and the absence of instrumental music, all seemed aesthetically unsatisfying to Jews who were acquainted with Christian forms of worship. In response, some of the *piyyutim* were omitted, liturgical music in a contemporary idiom was composed, and in Mantua an organ was installed in the synagogue. The use of Hebrew as the language of prayer was seen as an obstacle to full participation in the worship, and in 1522 the first Spanish translation of the liturgy was published in Ferrara. These early reforms had little direct influence in other countries, where social conditions were different. In due course, however, similar considerations led to analogous developments in Germany, Holland, and other parts of western and central Europe. Translations of the liturgy were made, both privately and under official auspices, in the course of the eighteenth century, and in 1796 a new synagogue was opened in Amsterdam in which many of the *piyyutim* were omitted from the service and sermons were delivered in Dutch. In Germany various initiatives in the early nineteenth century bore their first significant fruit in the dedication of the Hamburg temple in 1818. The services in the new temple were to be held according to a 'dignified and well-ordered ritual', with choral singing accompanied by an organ, and with a sermon in German. A few years later, similar reforms were instituted for the first time in the United States, in Charleston, South Carolina (at that time one of the foremost Jewish centres of North America). In London a reformed congregation was instituted in 1840: it published a prayer book the following year, and opened its first synagogue in 1842.

Liturgical reform is commonly associated with the more extreme modernist movements, such as Reform Judaism in America, or in Britain the Reform movement and the more radical Liberal movement which founded its first synagogue in 1910. It would be more realistic, however, to see it as a common feature of all the modernist trends, and at the same time to recognize that its progress has been far from rapid, consistent or unchallenged even on the Reform wing. Changes have come about, where they have, in a piecemeal and somewhat haphazard way, and almost always in the face of conservative opposition, even in Reform synagogues. (The Reform synagogue in London was described by the novelist Israel Zangwill, at the end of the nineteenth century, as 'a body which has stood still for fifty years admiring its past self'.) Nor is it easy to generalize about the promoters of reform or the resistance to it: sometimes the initiative for change has come from above, from the intellectual leadership, and met with opposition from more conservative congregations; sometimes demands for reform emanating from the congregations have been blocked or hampered by the rabbinate. Furthermore, although in retrospect reform is commonly seen as a 'package' of consistent and clearly-defined proposals, in fact it comprises a variety of disparate elements, arising from different causes (social or cultural, aesthetic or theological), and provoking a variety of responses. The result, over a long period of development, has been, on the one hand, a considerable measure of agreement within modernist Judaism as a whole, and on the other hand a great deal of conflict and dissent.

The area in which the greatest measure of agreement was achieved was the improvement in what was seen as the dignity and decorum of public worship. The casual and often unruly character of traditional synagogue worship is often illustrated by the disapproving comments of the diarist Samuel Pepys following his visit to the Sephardi synagogue in London in 1663. Pepy's visit took place during the celebrations of *Simhat Torah*, a festival on which a good deal of licence was traditionally granted to riotous behaviour. Nevertheless it is true that even the regular services left a great deal to be desired from a modern western aesthetic point of view. Their flavour can still be judged from traditionalist services today. There was a minimum of formal ceremonial. The service did not begin promptly at an advertised time, but tended to gather momentum gradually, the worshippers arriving in trickles, taking their places with some commotion, greeting their friends, engaging in often animated conversation and even heated arguments (sometimes occasioned by the sale of honours to the highest bidder during the service). The synagogue could easily appear to resemble a stock exchange rather than a house of prayer. That this was an old problem is clear from exhortations to decorum and attention, particularly during the reading of the Torah, in the traditional codes of conduct. In the early nineteenth century, in the face of increasingly outspoken dissatisfaction, steps finally began to be taken in many western European synagogues to remedy the situation. Committees were set up to review ways of improving decorum, certain practices (such as the sale of honours) were abolished, and gradually a more decorous and dignified form of worship was evolved. In Germany, throughout the nineteenth century, a whole series of

'Synagogue Orders' was issued in different places, to regulate the conduct and content of the services: typically they laid down that the service should begin at an advertised time, that officiants and worshippers should be clean and decently dressed, that worshippers should remain in their seats and refrain from making a noise or other disturbance during the service, that parents should be responsible for the good behaviour of children and that young children should not be brought to the synagogue. The details varied from place to place, and between Reform and Orthodox synagogues, but the general effect was similar: to make a form of worship that would be decorous and dignified, in the terms in which the words were understood by middle-class, western Jews, who were aware of western Christian habits of worship.

At the same time attention was paid to the music of the synagogue. The traditional service was conducted by a cantor (*hazzan*), who based himself on certain traditional patterns of chant but could exercise considerable freedom in his musical rendition. The traditional codes insist that the moral character and scholarship of the cantor are more important than his musical abilities, but it is evident from rabbinic denunciations of excessively histrionic performances that some cantors were more interested in the musical quality of their rendering of the prayers than in their religious content. Other critics complained that cantors were not musical enough. In the course of the nineteenth century cantors tended increasingly to have a musical education, and the influence of the church and the opera house made itself felt in the synagogue. Cantorial schools were set up, Jewish musical traditions were collected and studied, and several notable cantors either set traditional material in modern forms or composed new music for the synagogue in contemporary idioms. A result of this activity has been to raise the standard of cantorial music, and to increase the respect and admiration felt for individual cantors, some of whom, through the medium of recordings, have attracted a world-wide following. Many modernist synagogues, of all denominations, employ cantors, whose contribution is generally felt to enhance the appeal and quality of the services. On the other hand there has also been a trend to abolish the role of the cantor, and to have the service conducted by a reader, whether a professional (rabbi or minister), or a member of the congregation designated for the occasion. In Reform congregations which employ a cantor, his role is generally secondary to that of the reader. The early reformers stressed clarity of diction in the reading of the prayers, and to this end they tended to replace the traditional singsong chant by plain reading: this habit has persisted in Reform usage.

Another important development has been the introduction of choral music in the synagogue. In keeping with the general character of Orthodox worship, in which the sexes are segregated and the service is conducted exclusively by men, most Orthodox synagogues have opted for a male choir, with or without boys' voices. But mixed choirs are now a common feature of Reform and Conservative synagogues, and are not entirely unknown in Orthodox synagogues. However, many congregations have shown a preference for congregational singing (which has long been a feature of oriental synagogues and Hasidic worship), rather than a virtuoso performance by the cantor or choir, which has an inherent tendency to dominate the service, discouraging active participation by the congregation.

A more controversial question than the introduction of a choir was that of the organ. Its opponents argued that it was an aping of Christian custom, and that for a Jewish organist to play on the Sabbath would be an infringement of the Sabbath rest. Under the influence of the Hamburg temple (where the organ was played by a Christian), the Reformed Society of Israelites in Charleston, South Carolina installed an organ in 1841; five years later the dispute about it was taken to the state Court of Errors and Appeals. Eventually the sound of the organ was heard in all American Reform temples, and in many Conservative synagogues as well. In Britain the organ was first introduced in the London Reform synagogue in 1859. In France and Italy it was even welcomed into Orthodox synagogues, at least for use at marriages and other weekday services.

Although the Talmud lays down that prayers may be said in any language, traditional Judaism had been unswervingly faithful to the use of Hebrew in the synagogue, with the exception of a few prayers which were customarily recited in Aramaic, the ancient vernacular. The translation of the liturgy, and the inclusion of a parallel translation in prayer books, which became increasingly common in the nineteenth century, was intended to help the worshippers to follow the service and understand the prayers; it was not the intention at first that the translation should be used in worship, still less that it should supplant the Hebrew. The proposal to admit vernacular prayers and hymns into the service was hotly debated by the German Reformers. At the rabbinical conference held at Frankfurt in 1845 a resolution declaring that the use of Hebrew was not essential in public worship was adopted by a narrow majority, and was followed immediately by a unanimous decision to retain it for the time being out of regard for the feelings of the older generation. It was this cautious move in the direction of reform which provoked the withdrawal of Zacharias Frankel, one of the founders of the Conservative stream of modernism, who insisted that Hebrew was an indispensable element in Jewish life. Eventually prayers in the vernacular were introduced in many Reform synagogues, but with feelings running high on both sides change tended to be cautious. As late as 1896 a proposal by the ministers of the Reform synagogue in London to increase the very modest amount of English in the service was rejected. In America there was less opposition, and the use of Hebrew was reduced to a minimum or even eliminated completely in many Reform congregations (although it has undergone a remarkable recovery in this century). Even Conservative synagogues now commonly have some prayers or readings in the vernacular. While Orthodox congregations have generally been faithful to Hebrew, they often allow some prayers (for example, the prayer for the government) to be said in the vernacular. The retention or reintroduction of Hebrew in the synagogue, which runs counter to the trend in the church, has been notably strengthened by the revival of Hebrew as a spoken language in Israel. In fact, many Ashkenazi congregations have adopted the Sephardi-based Israeli pronunciation of Hebrew, in preference to their own traditional pronunciation.

But if vernacular worship was not introduced without stiff opposition, there was less objection to vernacular preaching, which was also one of the demands of the German Reform. Although preaching had apparently not been a feature of traditional German Jewish worship, elsewhere in the Jewish world it was not unknown. In antiquity it was common to expound the scriptural readings; sermons were delivered in Spanish in seventeenth-century Amsterdam, and they were a regular feature of synagogue services in Italy. The German sermon soon became a high-point of the modernist service in Germany, not only in

Reform temples but also in Orthodox synagogues, with the keen support of the Orthodox leader S. R. Hirsch. It was seen as an important way of making the services more interesting and attractive, as well as promoting the ideas of the modernist rabbis. In London sermons in English began to be delivered in the early nineteenth century, and in the latter part of the century preaching became an important part of the work of the new-style Anglo-Jewish ministers. It was encouraged by the Ashkenazi chief rabbi N. M. Adler, himself a powerful preacher, who was the guiding spirit behind the establishment in 1855 of Jews' College, a modern rabbinical seminary which had the training of preachers as one of its foremost aims. In America, too, the sermon became a prominent feature of the service, and a strong tradition of Jewish preaching was established.

Also among the demands of those who wished to make the service of the synagogue more attractive to western Jews was a plea that it should be shortened. The major services of the traditional synagogue, that is the morning services for Sabbaths and festivals, had a timeless quality, beginning early in the morning and continuing until well past midday. One of the proposals of the founders of the London Reform synagogue in 1840 was that the Sabbath morning service should be abbreviated so as to last no longer than two and a half hours. The reformers saw in the length of the service an obstacle to sincere devotion, and one of the main causes of the lack of decorum to which they took such strong exception. On the other hand, their concern for a dignified rendering of the prayers and readings, and their enthusiasm for musical embellishment, could only have the effect of lengthening the service still further.

Among the obvious candidates for omission were many of the medieval *piyyutim*. Their inclusion in the service in the first place had been opposed by many of the leading Geonim, and they had had their critics throughout the Middle Ages. Maimonides, for instance, in language strongly reminiscent of that of the modern reformers, categorizes them as 'the major cause for the lack of devotion and for the frivolity of the masses which leads them to talk during the prayer'; he adds the complaint that some of them are the work of poets who were not scholars. Both the language and the ideas of these poetic elaborations of the liturgy tend to be obscure, and their didactic content, it could be argued, had been rendered obsolete by the reintroduction of the sermon. They were progressively pruned out of the Reform liturgies, and eventually out of the Conservative and many of the Orthodox liturgies as well. Other omissions recommended themselves too on grounds of obscurity, or on grounds of unnecessary repetition. But inevitably, given the spirit of the age, once the door had been opened to the revision of the liturgy the question arose of the theological justification for some of the traditional prayers (particularly since the translation of the prayer book had made their meaning more obvious to the ordinary worshipper). This was the concern that was placed at the forefront by the American rabbi Samuel Adler, replying to a request for advice from the founder of the first Reform temple in Chicago in 1860:

The first and most important step for such a congregation to take is to free its service of shocking lies, to remove from it the mention of things and wishes which we would not utter if it had to be done in an intelligible manner. Such are, the lamentation about oppression and persecution, the petition for the restoration of the sacrificial cult, for the return to Palestine, the hope for a personal Messiah, and for the resurrection of the body. In the second place, to eliminate fustian and exaggeration, and, in the third place, to make the service clear, intelligible, instructive, and inspiring.

The topics specifically singled out for excision by Adler are those which, by general consent, western Jews of his day felt least able to pray for with heartfelt sincerity. But was that sufficient reason to remove them from the liturgy? There were many rabbis and liturgical reformers who felt that it was: the overriding consideration was that the worshipper should understand what he prayed and pray with honesty and sincerity. Others objected to such doctrinal doctoring of the prayers, whether from loyalty to tradition or from a fear that, once the doors were opened to such changes made from a standpoint of literalism and rationality, there would be no end to the revisions that would be demanded. Theological reform of the prayers was therefore conducted on a piecemeal and somewhat haphazard basis. Reform congregations excised some of the disputed passages while retaining others, or retained them in the Hebrew while paraphrasing them in a more acceptable form in the translation. In the revised editions of the prayer book that poured from the presses in the course of the nineteenth century, the general trend was for Reform prayer books to remove or rephrase the offending prayers, and for Orthodox prayer books to retain them, perhaps with very minor revisions. The American Conservative prayer books have accepted the principle of revision, but applied it very cautiously, relying where possible on poetic interpretation, imaginative translation, or additional notes.

It should not be thought that prayer book revision has tended only in the direction of abbreviation and deletion, although this has certainly been the dominant trend. In fact the shortening of the service has actually allowed some scope for new liturgical composition. Even the Orthodox prayer books contain some new prayers, although the additions are very limited. The Conservative and Reform prayer books, however, have incorporated a wealth of new material, either drawn from external sources or specially composed for the purpose. In the prayer books of the more radical movements, American Reform and British Liberal Judaism, old and new prayers are blended in almost equal proportions. These prayer books, together with the recently revised prayer book of the more conservative British Reform movement, also offer the innovation of alternative services, with the aim of making the worship more interesting and varied.

The reformers' aim of shortening the services was directed in the main at the Sabbath and festival morning service, as we have said. In the case of the evening services, they have actually tended in the opposite direction. The traditional evening service is very short, held at sunset and attracting mainly men, who then disperse to their homes to join their families for a festive meal. In 1866 the notable American reformer Isaac M. Wise of Cincinnati instituted a later, longer Friday evening service with a sermon. Wise was disturbed by the tendency among reformers of preaching at a Sunday morning service, in response to a serious decline in attendance on Sabbath morning. The after-dinner Friday evening service proved a great success: it was eventually adopted in most Reform and Conservative, and even many Orthodox, synagogues. Another widely-accepted innovation among Ashkenazim is a service to commemorate the dead, inserted into the worship on the Day of Atonement and the three festivals. Such commemorations were not unknown in traditional Judaism, but they were very brief, and in some rites were limited to the Day of Atonement or entirely lacking. The modern memorial service is more elaborate, and has become a prominent feature of the festival and Atonement Day services, attracting large numbers of people into the synagogue.

Far more controversial was the proposal to abolish the observance of a second day of the festivals, which is a rabbinic, not a biblical, institution. Its abolition was one of the early reforms of the London Reform congregation founded in 1840. In 1868 the British Chief Rabbi declined to follow suit, and although his refusal did not put an end to debate on the subject, it has remained definitive for Orthodoxy. In America the second day has been abolished in the Reform movement, but is retained by the Conservative and Orthodox. In Israel it has never been observed, except in the case of New Year; in fact there have been moves to restore the second day of New Year in some congregations in the diaspora as well.

To summarize, the overall effect of the reforms has been to achieve a more dignified and at the same time a more highly organized service. The superficial differences between the synagogue and the church have been smoothed out, if not removed completely: the use of Hebrew, which is staging a comeback even in the more radical congregations, is one striking difference; another is the segregation of men and women in Orthodox and some Conservative synagogues, and the wearing of a hat, or at least a skullcap, and the *tallit* or prayer-shawl. The synagogue has become, in a sense, 'professionalized', with larger synagogues employing a number of full-time or part-time officiants and musicians, as well as involving members of the congregation on a regular basis in supervising the conduct of the services and participating in the choir. The changes have their advantages and their disadvantages. On the one hand the aesthetic appeal of the services has been greatly increased, and they have been made easier to follow and to understand, more accessible to the wider Jewish public and particularly to women (who in Reform congregations at least can now participate on an equal basis with men). On the other hand they have tended to become somewhat remote and even theatrical, encouraging worshippers to become spectators rather than active participants. The fervour and warmth of the traditional service have been sacrificed in favour of decorum and elegance. In recent decades there has been a reaction, however, against this excess. With the decline of city-centre synagogues in favour of suburban congregations, and the arrival of new members nurtured on traditional forms of worship, there has been a certain relaxation in the formality of the modernist worship, with more congregational participation, the reintroduction of various traditional rituals, and some influence from the more passionate Hasidic worship. These new changes have affected the different types of congregation in different ways, but the general trend has been in the same direction: Reform worship has become more like Conservative, while the dividing line between Orthodox and traditionalist worship has become blurred (some Orthodox congregations even preferring the denomination 'traditional'). These latest developments highlight the fact, already mentioned, that liturgical reform is not a single, consistent package, but rather an attitude of mind: an openness to change and a sensitivity to outside influences and to the needs and wishes of the congregation.

4

The Biblical Tradition

Blessed are you, Lord our God, eternal King, who has
given us true Torah, and planted eternal life in our midst.
Blessed are you, Lord, Giver of the Torah.
Blessing after the reading of the Torah

The highlight of the major services of the synagogue is the
reading of the Torah. A handwritten parchment scroll containing
the Five Books of Moses is reverently opened and a designated
portion is read, followed by the *Haftara*, a reading from the
prophetic books. Worthy members of the congregation are
honoured by being called to take part in this ceremony, and it is
by participating in the public reading that a Jewish child today
marks his attainment of religious majority on the occasion of
his Barmitzvah. It is an impressive and much-loved ritual,
accompanied by appropriate blessings and gestures, and when
the scroll is held aloft and shown to the congregation they chant
the words, 'This is the Torah which Moses placed before the
children of Israel.'

In the course of a year the Torah is read from beginning to end,
and each Sabbath takes its name from its appointed reading. The
cycle ends and immediately begins again in the autumn, at the
festival of *Simhat Torah* or 'Rejoicing for the Torah'. This
popular festival marks the end of a period of festivals whose
dominant mood is solemn and earnest, and as if by way of relief
after such solemnity the mood of *Simhat Torah* is one of
unconfined joy. The scrolls are processed round the synagogue,
at first with some semblance of dignity, but then with ever
increasing joyfulness as they are passed from hand to hand amid
songs and dances, while the children wave specially prepared
flags. In some places it is still the custom to extend the procession
out of the synagogue and into the streets. The early summer
festival of *Shavuot*, a more restrained occasion than *Simhat
Torah*, commemorates the giving of the Torah: the appointed

Torah reading is the section describing the revelation at Sinai and the giving of the Ten Commandments.

In addition to all these public celebrations, the Bible is ever-present in all aspects of Jewish life and thought. It contributes much of the text of the liturgy, and material for sermons and speeches. It is the basis of religious education and religious law, and it is also read as a national epic and as a sourcebook of moral and theological teachings. It is no exaggeration to say that it is the most treasured heritage of the Jewish people, and for countless Jews down the ages it has been far more than this: the definitive revelation of God's will for all mankind.

The Bible is known in Hebrew as *Tanakh*, which is an acronym of the names of its three parts: *Torah* ('Instruction'), *Neviim* ('Prophets'), and *Ketuvim* ('Writings'). This threefold division, which differs from the usual Christian arrangement of the books, is very old, and is thought to reflect the stages in which the text was codified. It still influences the way in which the sections are regarded, and the use which is made of them. The first section, the *Torah*, is regarded as the most sacred and authoritative: in synagogue it is read in a series of continuous lections from texts written by hand on specially prepared parchment scrolls. The lections from the Prophets are only selected excerpts, read from printed texts, while the books of the Writings, with a few exceptions, do not figure in the public readings.

The text of the Hebrew Bible as it is found in printed editions today is remarkably homogeneous. It is the result of a process of editing which dates back centuries, and was essentially complete by the tenth century. The editors are known as Masoretes, from the Hebrew word *masorah* which is associated with the word *masoret*, 'tradition'. The so-called Masoretic text is thus a traditional text, a text produced by tradition and hallowed by traditional use. Modern research has brought to light many textual variants which existed in ancient times, before the Masoretic process had produced a universally accepted Hebrew edition. These discoveries are of great help in understanding the early history of the text and the meaning of difficult passages. But so far as the religious use of the Bible is concerned, in public readings and preaching, Jews have remained ineradicably attached to the Masoretic text.

The Bible is still read and taught in the original Hebrew, and this attachment to the Hebrew Bible is certainly one of the factors which have encouraged the retention of Hebrew as a language of prayer and study among Jews. But Jews have not been averse to making and using translations of the biblical books as well. The oldest translation is the Septuagint, a Greek version which was made over a long period of time, beginning in the third century BCE. It was very widely employed by Jews in the Graeco-Roman period, but eventually fell out of use. It only survives today because it was taken up into a living Christian tradition, the same tradition to which we owe the survival of many other ancient Jewish works in Greek, such as the extensive writings of the historian Josephus and the philosopher Philo, or the miscellaneous compositions known as the Apocrypha and Pseudepigrapha. In contrast, the Aramaic translation, known as the Targum, which is in some ways more of a paraphrase or exposition than a literal translation, continued to be copied and studied in scholarly circles, even though Aramaic has long since ceased to be a living language for all but a tiny minority of Jews. It is still printed in traditional editions of the Hebrew Bible. The precise date of the Targum is not known, in fact in a sense it has no fixed date, for the Targum is actually a tradition in itself: it exists in several different texts, and they are the written remains of a rich oral tradition of biblical translation and exposition which developed over centuries. The Bible was later translated into many other languages as the need arose. But even though translations are of enormous benefit in a society in which Hebrew is not the first language, no translation has ever ousted the Hebrew from its pride of place as the authentic sacred text. At this point the Jewish and Christian traditions, which share so much in their common attachment to the biblical writings, definitively part company.

Every sacred text needs to be continuously interpreted and explained if it is to keep its place in a living religious tradition. The Hebrew Bible is no exception. The Bible itself contains traces of such interpretation, and in a sense almost the whole of the subsequent Jewish scholarly tradition can be seen as a commentary on the sacred text, in which each generation grapples with what it has received and makes it vocal and meaningful for its own conditions.

The activity of the ancient rabbis was very largely devoted to the study and practical application of the biblical teachings. This activity took many forms, but the most highly developed was the study of biblical law and its harmonization with law deriving from other sources, such as established custom and the decisions of lawcourts. Because of the theological axiom that God's will was perfectly revealed at Sinai, there was a strongly felt need to find biblical prooftexts which would support practices and decisions from whatever source they derived. Rabbinic education inculcated an encyclopaedic knowledge of the biblical text, as well as methods of argument adapted to establishing the biblical legitimacy of later practice. From this exercise sprang the lists of hermeneutical principles, or admissible forms of argument. One list, attributed to a second-century rabbi, enumerates no less than thirty-two different forms of argument which may be used in extending or defining biblical rules. The Talmudic literature consists very largely of records of rabbinic discussions on matters of law and practice, in which a central concern is the establishment of the biblical basis of each decision.

Side by side with the writings which make up the Talmud, the ancient rabbis have also left us a rich legacy of reflection and exposition on biblical topics in the body of works known collectively as the Midrash. Unlike the Talmud, in which the material is organized according to subject matter, the Midrash is presented in terms of the biblical text itself. Some of the works take the form of a running commentary on a biblical book, while others present homilies on the texts selected for public reading on various Sabbaths and festivals. The overall effect in either case is similar: the Midrash is not a continuous and coherent commentary by a single author, but a compendium of expositions, some of which are attributed to named rabbis while others are anonymous. Here again we see clearly the working of tradition as a guiding concept. Each of the named authorities in the rabbinic writings is a link in the chain of tradition, and positive merit is attached to citing a statement accurately in the name of its author; indeed we sometimes find a sequence of two or more rabbis who each quoted the saying in the name of his teacher. But ultimately what is important is the tradition itself, not the individual minds which shaped it, and consequently we do not find in the rabbinic literature, as we do as a matter of course in the Christian patristic literature of the same period, commentaries and treatises which are entirely the work of one teacher and are handed down under his name. Later on in the tradition attempts were made to identify the main authors or the final editors of the rabbinic compilations, just as the rabbis themselves sought to identify the authors of the biblical books. These attempts are part of an effort to understand and codify the history of the tradition as a tradition; they do not indicate a desire to relate the works in question to the biography, the particular genius or the historical situation of the supposed author.

The Midrashic literature is a traditional literature in another sense, too. The works were produced over a long period of time, beginning perhaps in the second century CE and continuing until at least the twelfth century. During this long period the form and content of the works remained remarkably constant—so much so that there are serious disagreements among scholars about the dating of some of the texts. Some of the works are so similar that they appear to be almost, but not quite, the same work. And even works which are quite different repeat long passages from each other. Clearly what has happened is that each Midrashic work is a compilation of traditional material, not in any real sense a new creation. An analogous process has occurred in the case of the Talmud and the Targum: what has been preserved in writing represents a frozen moment in the history of a long and rich tradition, and no doubt a great deal more has perished forever.

Long before the creative period of Midrash came to an end, a new approach to the interpretation of the Bible had begun. Like so much else in the Jewish scholarly tradition the new beginning may be associated with the name of Saadya: not only did he translate the Bible into Arabic, he also wrote commentaries on a number of biblical books. Whereas the Midrash is largely homiletical in character, and frequently departs a long way from the plain meaning of the scriptural text, Saadya, who took a deep interest in Hebrew grammar and philology, adopts a far more straightforward and scientific approach. His work laid the foundations for a tradition of biblical commentary which is one of the enduring achievements of Jewish scholarship. The Jewish commentators exercised an important influence on Latin Christian biblical scholarship, and even today their work cannot be ignored by modern biblical critics.

The best known of the medieval Jewish commentators is Rashi

(1040–1105), whose academy at Troyes in Champagne attracted students from far and wide. Rashi's commentary on the Bible draws freely on the Midrash, but his approach is entirely different. In simple style he comments on each verse in turn, concentrating on explaining difficulties and obscurities rather than reading extraneous ideas into the text. His work acquired enormous popularity, partly because it could be used for teaching children. It was widely copied and studied, and was in due course one of the first Hebrew works to be printed; it became itself the object of numerous commentaries (or rather supercommentaries), and is often found printed in editions of the Hebrew Bible alongside the biblical text.

Another notable commentator is the Spanish scholar Abraham Ibn Ezra (1092–1167). Ibn Ezra's commentary has never achieved quite the same popularity as that of Rashi, which is not surprising since it is a much more demanding work to read. Whereas Rashi's simple Hebrew can be followed by anyone with a modestly competent knowledge of the language, and his aim is to familiarize the reader with the traditional interpretation of the text, Ibn Ezra is an exact and exacting scholar, with a keen interest in philology and philosophy, who hardly lets slip an opportunity to expand on an unusual grammatical form or a philosophical idea. And whereas Rashi is content to follow Midrashic interpretations, Ibn Ezra does not hesitate to reject the traditional interpretation if it conflicts with his own scientific understanding of the text. At times he even permits himself obliquely worded comments which depart abruptly from traditional beliefs about the character of the Bible. He is evidently sceptical, for example, about the idea that the whole Torah was written by Moses, and he is also the first critic to suggest that the book of Isaiah was the work of more than one author. His commentary is one of the finest monuments of medieval Jewish scholarship, and both in its general method and its individual insights it anticipates more modern developments in biblical criticism.

The growth of the science of Hebrew grammar, under Arabic influence, had an effect on poetry as well as on biblical scholarship. Synagogal poetry has its origins in Byzantine Palestine, and the early poets, although they did not make use of the formal features of biblical poetry, evince a fascination for biblical language and ideas. Ibn Ezra himself criticized the traditional poetry for its linguistic obscurity and grammatical inaccuracy, and the Hispano-Arabic Jewish culture to which he belonged gave rise to a new style of Hebrew poetry, making use of Arabic metres and genres, but also characterized by a purer Hebrew diction and an astonishing mastery of the language in all its richness. All the best medieval Hebrew poetry displays an intimate familiarity with the language and thought of the Bible, and it relies, for a full appreciation of its subtleties, on a similar familiarity among its hearers. The best-known poets also left their mark as scholars in other fields, and scholars commonly tried their hand at writing poetry. Poetry and scholarship were thus continually nourishing each other, and the common ground between them was the Hebrew Bible.

The biblical basis of medieval Jewish culture can be seen not only in the poetry but in every aspect of life and thought from the most exalted to the most homely. Education was not reserved for a cultural or religious élite, but was regarded as a fundamental requirement for all (at least for all males, since in keeping with prevailing medieval prejudice it was thought to be wasted on females). 'These words which I command you today shall be in your mind: you shall teach them to your children and talk about them at home and abroad, sleeping and waking.' This biblical injunction, which was repeated twice a day in prayer, was taken as a solemn obligation to instruct children in Torah (in its broadest sense). And since throughout the Middle Ages Jews were denied access to other centres of learning (with the sole and partial exception of medical schools), the syllabus of their own schools and academies naturally dominated the character of the whole culture. The twin pillars of this syllabus were the Bible and the Talmud, the Bible being taught (with Rashi's commentary) to children, and the Talmud to adults. At the more general level it was the Bible that predominated, reinforced by the regular public readings in the synagogue.

Even where the surrounding culture did impinge on the self-contained universe of Jewish scholarship the result was often to highlight the role of the Bible. One obvious example is in the religious disputations, in which spokesmen for Judaism and Christianity were called on to debate in public the rival claims of their respective faiths. Here the Bible seemed to provide a natural common ground, and the arguments frequently focused on the interpretation of biblical texts virtually to the exclusion of other topics. But an equally important area was the work of the philosophers, who were engaged in a constant dialogue with thinkers who belonged to the other monotheistic faiths. In the writings of the Jewish philosophers rational arguments are interwoven with discussions of biblical texts. Moses Maimonides' *Guide for the Perplexed*, for example, which is acknowledged as the masterwork of medieval Jewish philosophy, can be read as a kind of philosophical commentary on the most difficult passages of the Bible.

The fundamental role of the Bible in Jewish culture endured so long as the Jewish Middle Ages lasted, that is until political emancipation broke down the educational and social barriers between Jews and Gentiles and introduced the mass of Jews to secular studies and external ways of thinking. Even then the process of change was a gradual one for many people, as assimilation came about only slowly in the larger and more traditional centres of Jewish population and insofar as the general culture into which the Jews were being absorbed continued to be dominated by the Christian biblical tradition. It is ironical that it was a Jew, Baruch Spinoza (1632–77), who was one of the founding fathers of the rational enlightenment which undermined the authority of the Bible in European culture. Spinoza took up the criticisms of the traditional view of the Mosaic authorship of the Torah which had been advanced cryptically by Abraham Ibn Ezra and developed them as part of a thoroughgoing critique of the traditional standpoint. He cites the evidence of the Bible itself to show that it was composed much later than the time of Moses, and he challenges the much-vaunted purity and accuracy of the textual tradition. With hindsight he can be seen as one of the founders of the modern science of biblical criticism. But his critique of traditional Judaism went much further than this. There is no room for revelation, as it was traditionally understood, in his strictly rational system, and he can only consider the Bible as the word of God insofar as it contains the universal human religion which can be understood independently through the faculty of reason. The compromise between philosophy and religious tradition which had been pursued by thinkers throughout the Middle Ages was barely possible in such a system.

Spinoza's thought had little immediate impact on Jews (he was expelled from the Portuguese Jewish community of Amsterdam in 1656), but it was to have an enormous influence on western European ideas generally. On the political plane, Spinoza had been a proponent of a liberal state tolerating freedom of thought. As this idea slowly gained ground Jewish intellectuals were gradually admitted into the debates of western thinkers who were becoming increasingly polarized between anti-religious rationalism and religious reaction. This tension was naturally fraught with dangers for the Jewish participants. On the one hand they could only benefit from a more liberal intellectual climate, which also held out the hope of a separation of Church and State which might relieve the Jewish communities of the serious disabilities from which they suffered under Christian rule. But on the other hand as religious Jews they could not ally themselves wholeheartedly with an essentially anti-religious movement.

Moses Mendelssohn (1729–86) was the first major Jewish thinker to emerge in this new period of rapprochement, and his attitude to the Bible is significant both in itself and in relation to its influence on those who followed him. Mendelssohn was a convinced rationalist, and his general approach to religion is not dissimilar to that of Spinoza. But whereas Spinoza's rationalism had led him away from Judaism, Mendelssohn identified himself firmly as a member of the Jewish people and accepted the eternally binding force of Jewish law. In his most influential and enduring book, *Jerusalem*, Mendelssohn allied Judaism to the religion of reason, and drew a fundamental distinction between Judaism and Christianity:

I recognize no eternal truths except those which can not only be comprehended by the human intellect but also demonstrated and confirmed by man's faculties . . . I consider this view an essential aspect of the Jewish religion and believe that this teaching represents one of the characteristic differences between Judaism and Christianity. To sum it up in one sentence: I believe Judaism knows nothing of a *revealed religion* corresponding to the way Christians understand this term. The Israelites possess a *divine legislation*: laws, commandments, statutes, rules of conduct, instruction in God's will and in what they are to do to attain temporal and eternal happiness. Moses, in a miraculous and supernatural way, revealed to them these laws and commandments, but not dogmas, saving truths or self-evident propositions. These the Lord reveals to us as well as to all other men at all times through nature and events, never through the spoken or written word.

For Mendelssohn, then, Judaism lays no claim to any exclusive religious truth: on the contrary, it upholds and preserves the universal values of rational religion. But the biblical laws, which for Spinoza had a purely political function limited to the existence of a self-governing Jewish state, he considers to be revealed by God and of eternal value. In this way Mendelssohn attempted to separate the two worlds in which he lived and to eliminate the conflict between them. It was a compromise which was not particularly successful: western Jewish thought in the course of the nineteenth century tended to become polarized between the belief in the traditional integrity and divine authority of the Bible and a faith in reason, progress and universal values. But against the background of its times it can be seen as a remarkable pioneering effort, and Mendelssohn is generally regarded as the founder of modern Jewish religious thought. Less well remembered nowadays is his role as the father of the popular Bible commentary. Mendelssohn published a German translation of the Bible (in Hebrew characters), accompanied by a commentary, written by a team of scholars, which sought to make the best insights of the Jewish exegetical tradition accessible to modern readers. This commentary, the *Biur*, was written in Hebrew—an ill-judged choice, since in the process of social integration for which Mendelssohn himself had laboured the western Jews soon abandoned Hebrew for most purposes in favour of the vernacular languages. But this type of commentary came to be widely imitated in a variety of other languages, and became an important instrument in spreading a knowledge of traditional Jewish exegesis combined with modern comments from a broad range of sources.

The revolutionary theories of the modern biblical critics were as disturbing for Jews as they were for Christians. In particular the quest for different documentary sources within the Torah and the redating of some other parts of the Bible (including for example a very late date for some of the Psalms, traditionally attributed to King David) threatened to undermine completely the traditional rabbinic view of the integrity and authorship of the biblical books. The battle about biblical criticism was fiercely waged, and it divided Jewish scholars along lines which do not coincide as closely as one might expect with the emerging schools of religious thought. Several of the leading figures in the nascent Orthodox movement were quick to realize the possibilities of modern biblical criticism, and were no less enthusiastic than pioneers of Reform in proposing emendations of the text. But as the confrontation between Orthodox and Reform rabbis became more outspoken, a dogmatic rejection of modern approaches to biblical criticism became more pronounced on the Orthodox side. The new attitude is best encapsulated in the public questions addressed in 1853 by Samson Raphael Hirsch, rabbi at Frankfurt am Main and a leading opponent of Reform, to the founders of a new-style rabbinic seminary at Breslau. Hirsch was actually a firm believer in bringing Judaism out of the ghetto and in taking advantage of modern methods of education and research, while Zacharias Frankel, who had been invited to be the principal of the new seminary, was a rather traditional modernist. But as the spokesman of the new Orthodoxy Hirsch evidently felt called on to make a strong statement on this occasion. His opening questions were:

What will revelation mean in the proposed seminary? For Orthodox Judaism it is the direct word of the one, personal God to man, and 'God spoke to Moses' is a simple, supernatural fact, just as one man speaks to another. Do the leaders of the seminary acknowledge this Orthodox belief?

What will the Bible mean in the proposed seminary? Orthodox Judaism believes in the divine authenticity of the Bible, and knows nothing of the various authors of the Pentateuch, nor of Pseudo-Isaiah, nor of Maccabean songs under the name of David, nor of Solomon's Ecclesiastes from the time of the Second Temple, and so forth. What do the leaders of the seminary say about the authenticity of the Bible?

This outspoken challenge to modern approaches to the Bible is important because it has continued to influence Orthodox Judaism to this day. Whereas the other streams in modernist Judaism, both radical Reform and the more conservative stance of which Frankel was a pioneer, have been willing to accept modern research on its own terms, even if they have resisted some of its more extreme trends, Orthodoxy has always inclined to put forward the rejection of biblical criticism as a fundamental issue of faith. This has not prevented the emergence of some very fine Orthodox biblical scholars, although their research has tended to be conducted along cautious and very conservative lines. But it has had the effect of allying Orthodoxy, which is in other respects a modernist movement, with the forces of anti-modernist traditionalism (in fact

nowadays the term Orthodox is often applied without distinction
to all the fundamentalist elements in Judaism), while cutting it off
from the Conservative trend with which it otherwise has a great
deal in common. This is one of the rare instances of a basically
theological division in Judaism.

Those Jews who reject the fundamentalist approach are left
with the problem of making sense of the concept of revelation
and of the biblical tradition within a world view which is fundamentally different from that in which the traditional ideas developed. Modern biblical critics agree that the biblical writings were
composed over a long period of time and that their authors lived
in different places and under different social and political conditions. Many different religious viewpoints are represented within
the pages of the Bible. Even the Torah, the 'Five Books of Moses'
which for the fundamentalist were revealed intact at Sinai, is seen
as a composite creation in which several different strands can be
disentangled. As for the Hebrew text in current use, it is a relatively late creation which does not agree in every detail with the
oldest manuscripts we have and may be very different from the
original form of the text. It is hardly surprising that biblical
criticism has posed a severe challenge to modern Judaism. But its
fruits are not entirely negative. Textual and linguistic studies
have shed fascinating new light on the early forms of the text and
its original meaning, while literary and historical investigations
have enormously enriched our understanding of the processes by
which Judaism developed from its earliest beginnings to the stage
it had reached by the end of the biblical period. The problem is
how to accommodate the new insights into a religious tradition
which is essentially traditional.

The problem is not insuperable, and once the idea of tradition
is itself understood and accepted even the clash between funda-
mentalists and biblical critics may appear as peripheral to
Judaism. Each generation, as we have seen, has read the Bible
and responded to it in the light of its own knowledge and its own
needs. Bible here means not just the written text, but the text as
understood and expounded by previous generations. And each
new response, each new interpretation, is potentially capable of
becoming part of the tradition. Understood in this way, the Bible
is neither the Bible of the‑fundamentalists, unchanging and
inerrant, nor the Bible of the critics, human and remote. It is a

living tradition, in which modern scholarship can also take its rightful place.

This solution, which can claim powerful support in older Jewish tradition, was first formulated in the 1920s by Franz Rosenzweig, who with Martin Buber translated the Hebrew Bible into German. With the additional support of Buber's theology of response it has gained considerable ground in the intervening period. It should be observed that it involves a certain shift in the traditional understanding of revelation. Once the basic premises of modern biblical criticism are accepted, it becomes hard (not that it was ever very easy) to see the text itself as the vehicle of revelation. The Bible is the work of men: written by men, edited by men, and subject to a continuing process of interpretation by men. This is not a new idea. One of the early rabbis declared that 'The Torah speaks in the language of men', and the Talmud betrays an awareness that the Torah is constantly evolving. Revelation, according to this view, is to be sought not in the written words themselves, but in the events they describe, the ideas they convey, and, it could be argued, even in the response they evoke in human hearts and minds.

This approach also preserves, or rather restores, the idea of the unity of Torah, which was so dear to the rabbis. That there are apparent contradictions in the text of the Bible can hardly be denied: to the biblical critic they are valuable clues to the process of original authorship and redaction. An approach which accepts scientific criticism but is not dominated by it, focusing instead on the continuing tradition, does not find them unduly troubling. Rosenzweig underlined this idea of unity in a celebrated letter to a leader of German Orthodoxy:

We too translate the Torah as a single book. For us, too, it is the work of one spirit. Among ourselves we call him by the symbol which critical science is accustomed to use to designate its assumed redactor: R. But this symbol R we expand not into redactor but into *Rabbenu*. For he is our teacher; his theology is our teaching.

What Rosenzweig has in mind here is the problem of the unity of the written text. But the idea can be extended to encompass the tradition as a whole, including the Masoretes, the medieval commentators and the modern critics. Not that they all agree—far from it. The rabbis long ago accepted that each word of Torah can be interpreted in an infinite number of different ways. But all the different interpretations are themselves part of Torah, and the unity of the Torah derives from the essential unity of the tradition itself. In the words of an ancient teacher, 'These and those are the words of the living God.'

5

The Legal Tradition

> With eternal love do you love the house of Israel, your
> people: Torah and commandments, statutes and judg-
> ments have you taught us. Therefore, O Lord our God,
> on lying down and rising we shall think about your
> statutes and rejoice in the words of your Torah and your
> commandments for ever and ever. For they are our life
> and the length of our days: we shall meditate on them
> day and night. Never remove your love from us. Blessed
> are you, Lord, who loves his people Israel.
>
> From the Evening Service

The ceremony of *bar mitzvah* (for a boy) or *bat mitzvah* (for a
girl) is a high point in the life of any Jew, and an occasion for
celebration in every Jewish family. What it signifies is the ending
of childhood and the beginning of adult life, and this moment is
normally reached at the age of twelve in the case of a girl and
thirteen in the case of a boy. In the midst of the celebrations the
original meaning of the technical terms is easily lost sight of:
mitzvah means 'commandment', and to be an adult in Judaism,
to be the son (*bar*) or daughter (*bat*) of the commandment, is to
be fully responsible for one's actions and subject to the full force
of the law.

The concept of law has always played a central role in mainstream Judaism. Yet it is a role which is too easily exaggerated or
distorted. Judaism without law would possibly not be Judaism
(although this would be challenged by some schools of thought),
but a Judaism which is nothing but law would be a travesty of
Judaism. Nor is there in Judaism (as Christian polemists have
claimed) a contrast between law and love. On the contrary, as the
prayer quoted above shows, the two are intimately related. The
laws are a sign of God's love, and the study of the laws is a way of
reciprocating that love.

Hebrew has many words for 'law', and, as the prayer also
shows, the word 'Torah' can readily take its place among them;

indeed much of the content of Torah consists of commandments and regulations. But law is only one aspect of Torah, and, as we have already seen, its real meaning is 'teaching' or 'instruction'. The biblical word *mishpat* is closer to the idea of the English word 'law'; it is related to the word *shofet* which means 'judge'. Both these terms are current in modern Hebrew usage in Israel. In traditional Jewish usage, a word which more accurately reflects the idea of law is *din*: it can mean law in general, or a specific law. It also means 'justice' or 'judgment'. A Jewish lawcourt is called a *Bet Din*, and a rabbi acting as a judge is called a *dayyan*, from the same root. The word is also applied to justice as an attribute of God, and on hearing news of a death it is customary to bless God as the true *dayyan*. It is a word which is heavy with religious meaning.

But the Hebrew term which most closely corresponds to the English word 'law' (whether in a general sense or with the idea of a single regulation) is *halakhah*. The word *halakhah* is commonly derived from the root *halakh*, meaning 'walk', so that the word would mean something like the correct 'way' in which one should conduct oneself. This etymology has now been challenged in favour of a more formally legal origin, and indeed Halakhah as it has traditionally been understood has certainly carried a sense of a higher obligation than that deriving merely from accepted or acceptable human conduct. But even *halakhah* does not mean exactly the same as 'law'. In its widest sense it is applied, for example in the study of the ancient Jewish literature, to whatever is of practical application, in contrast to *aggadah*, non-practical matter including history and legend, science and folk-wisdom, and even speculative subjects having a bearing on practice such as theology and ethics. Halakhah includes within its scope both civil and criminal law and also religious regulations and precepts guiding human life in a less legal sense. An obvious illustration of this wide range is provided by the Ten Commandments, in which prohibitions of behaviour as diverse as theft, murder, polytheism and idolatry, false testimony and covetousness are accompanied by injunctions to respect one's parents and keep the Sabbath. The more developed halakhic codes regulate minute details of personal, social and religious life as well as propounding general principles for human behaviour.

Halakhah provides one of the outstanding examples of a tradi-

tion within Judaism. Indeed for many people Halakhah and
Jewish tradition are virtually synonymous, although many others
would contest this rather narrow definition of Jewish tradition. It
is certainly a tradition which has attracted some of the finest
minds over the centuries, and throughout the long middle period
of Jewish history halakhic studies constituted the core of higher
Jewish education. The halakhic literature is profuse, and
stretches in unbroken continuity from antiquity to the present.
Moreover, each element in the halakhic tradition, each legal
judgment or responsum, each religious or ritual decision, is formulated in terms of the antecedent tradition, so that Halakhah is
actually a tradition which is dominated by tradition, a tradition
in which the sense of tradition is uncommonly strong.

That is not to say that Halakhah is constant and unchanging.
On the contrary, like all legal traditions it is subject to a continuous process of adaptation to changing circumstances. The
Halakhah is in a real sense a living tradition: it responds to the
changing needs of real people, and in its turn it exerts an influence
on their lives. It is true that the academic study of Halakhah
covers a plethora of topics of little or no direct relevance to
contemporary life. But the purpose of such study is to show how
the original laws can be applied, ever more directly and minutely,
in the lives of human beings striving to guide their actions
according to the divine will as expressed in the Torah.

The history of Halakhah may be divided, like all Jewish
history, into three main sections.

The ancient period gave birth to what have remained ever since
the most important and authoritative halakhic texts, namely the
Torah and the Talmud. Both these documents contain a great
deal of aggadic or non-halakhic material, but their halakhic
ingredient constitutes the foundation of all subsequent Halakhah.
Neither document can be considered as a legal code. They both
contain an enormous mass of legal material, some of which represents earlier attempts at codification, and all of which has been
subjected to a complex process of editorial revision. The precise
relationship between the material in the Torah and the Talmud is
a subject which has been much discussed since early times, as has
the relative authority attaching to each class of material. Although
historically the Talmud is of a much later date than the Torah, the
tradition itself regards both as complementary components in a

single whole, referring (rather confusingly) to the legal elements of the Torah (sometimes termed the Mosaic Law) as the 'Written Torah' and to those of the Talmud as the 'Oral Torah'. The underlying idea is not so much that the teachings of the Talmud, after being formulated by the rabbis, were handed down for a time in unwritten form (although this idea is certainly often discussed), but rather that Moses received both parts at Sinai, and that the Oral Torah derived from that revelation equally with the Written Torah.

The root meaning of the world Talmud is 'study', and the phrase 'Talmud Torah' in Hebrew means 'study of the Torah', which is a religious obligation. 'It is a fine thing to combine Talmud Torah with a worldly occupation,' says a rabbinic maxim, 'because the combined labour involved leaves no time for sin.' ('Talmud Torah' can also mean a school where Torah is studied.) There are actually two Talmuds, the Palestinian Talmud (often called the Yerushalmi) and the Babylonian Talmud (or Bavli). Although the two Talmuds differ considerably in terms of their contents, there is a great deal of material which is common to both, and the basic organization of the two is the same. They start from the work known as the Mishnah, a compilation which evolved gradually in the course of the early rabbinic period (late first to late second century CE) and probably reached its present form in the first half of the third century. Each Talmud is set out as a sort of commentary (known as *Gemara*) on the text of the Mishnah: typically a passage of the Mishnah is quoted, and a detailed discussion (which may actually wander far from the content of the Mishnaic passage) follows. In a sense neither Talmud is complete, since they both contain long passages of Mishnah, extending to whole tractates, which are not provided with a *Gemara*. The Babylonian Talmud is much larger than the Palestinian, but the Palestinian Talmud contains a *Gemara* on several tractates of the Mishnah which have none in the Babylonian Talmud. For historical reasons which need not be gone into here, the Babylonian Talmud came to enjoy far greater. authority than the Palestinian, but both have been copied and studied continuously since late antiquity, and with the revival of rabbinic studies in Israel in recent times there has been renewed interest in the teachings of the Palestinian Talmud. It is convenient to refer to the whole of this literature as 'Talmud', even though the rabbinic scholar is well aware of the differences between the Mishnah, the Palestinian Talmud, and the Babylonian Talmud. One may also include under the heading 'Talmud' the work known as the Tosefta, which is similar in form to the Mishnah. Conventionally a distinction is drawn between the Talmud and the Midrash, because of an obvious difference in their formal arrangement and subject matter, but there is actually a small group of so-called 'halakhic midrashim' which, while they are arranged in the commentary-form of the Midrash, contain a preponderance of halakhic material.

The subject matter of the Talmud is arranged under six major headings, each subdivided into a number of tractates. The first heading, 'Seeds', is mainly concerned with agricultural laws, but it opens with a tractate devoted to prayers and blessings. Next comes 'Appointed Times', that is the regulations for Sabbaths, festivals and other special days. The third heading, 'Women', contains tractates on marriage, divorce and other aspects of personal status. 'Damages', the fourth section, is concerned with the civil and criminal law, while the remaining sections, 'Holy Things' and 'Purity', deal respectively with temple sacrifices and the rules of ritual impurity. These headings serve to define the interests of the Halakhah in early Rabbinic Judaism. It is interesting to note that the last two sections are virtually ignored in the *Gemara*, with the exception of the food laws and the rules concerning menstrual impurity, while the agricultural laws, which were only regarded as binding in the Land of Israel, are not dealt with systematically in the *Gemara* of the Babylonian Talmud. The implication is that the halakhists, despite their strong academic interests, were concerned primarily to elucidate the law in those areas which were of continuing practical significance. And indeed, although they frequently discuss biblical commandments and their hypothetical ramifications, they also often cite actual cases, arising out of the experience of the lawcourts or questions addressed to the rabbis in their capacity as academic lawyers. Moreover, the rabbis display a deep sensitivity to actual custom, *minhag*: there is even a saying that 'Custom annuls Halakhah', a reminder that Jewish law is not seen as only a divine revelation, but is rooted in the life of the people.

The ancient period comes to an end with the consolidation of Christian rule in Palestine and of Muslim rule in Babylonia, and these are the moments when the Palestinian and Babylonian Talmuds, respectively, appear to have been edited in their present form. The succeeding Middle Ages, during which the Jews lived under the constraints imposed by the Christian and Muslim political systems, saw the Halakhah developing along somewhat different paths, in terms both of emphasis and of the types of literature produced. Three main types of halakhic writing evolved. In the first place there are commentaries on the Talmud, of which the classic example is Rashi's commentary on the Babylonian Talmud. The commentaries are intended as a contribution to the study and teaching of the earlier texts. A related genre arising out of this study are the *hiddushim* or novellae, refining points of Halakhah on which the sources are unclear or inconsistent. The second main type of writing consists of responsa, replies by halakhic experts to questions addressed to them by local judges or communal leaders. There are estimated to be some 300,000 of these responsa, and they constitute the case law of the medieval Halakhah, exercising a vital formative influence on the evolution of the law. The third, and in some respects the most novel, type of literature are the codes.

The need for a codification of the Halakhah arose from the enormous and unwieldy bulk of the traditional material, both within the Talmud itself and in the subsequent literature. To reach a decision on the basis of this traditional material demanded in each individual case an enormous effort, which could in any case only be attempted by a lawyer with a very thorough and competent training. The temptation to reduce the traditional decisions to a manageable compendium was naturally very cogent. It was, however, strenuously resisted by many leading halakhists at various times, who insisted on the danger of separating the Halakhah from its sources. Precisely because Halakhah is a tradition, any decision needs to be made (they argued) on the basis of familiarity with the living tradition, and not by consulting a 'dead' codification. Consequently each of the great pioneering efforts of codification met with vigorous opposition, which effectively prevented the adoption of any standard and universally accepted code until virtually the end of the Middle Ages.

The codification of the Halakhah begins with early attempts at summarizing topics in the Talmud. The peak of this early phase of activity is the code of Isaac Alfasi, produced in the middle of the eleventh century. Like its predecessors it is arranged in the order of the Talmudic tractates, and deals only with topics still of practical application, omitting those areas of the Halakhah which only apply in the Land of Israel or in the existence of the Temple.

The next great code, the *Mishneh Torah* of Maimonides, is based on different principles. Maimonides aimed to include all the topics of the Halakhah, including those not of current application, and he arranged his material not in Talmudic order but on the basis of a new classification of the subject matter. He also deliberately omitted all reference to Talmudic sources, names of authorities and dissenting opinions, in the interests of producing a simple, straightforward code which could be readily used by anybody, and not only by halakhic specialists. He even devised a special, simple form of Hebrew for his code, as opposed to the Arabic in which he wrote his other works or the complex, formulaic Aramaic of the Talmud itself. While Maimonides' work was greatly admired in some quarters, in others he was sharply attacked for daring to sever the laws themselves from their background in the tradition. As a result his code never achieved its aim of superseding the detailed study of the tradition for practical purposes, even though it exerted a considerable influence on subsequent compilations.

Jacob ben Asher, in the fourteenth century, devised a new division of the subject matter of the Halakhah under four headings or 'rows' (whence the title of his code, *Arbaah Turim*, which means 'The Four Rows'). The first deals with daily life and the rituals connected with the Sabbath and the festivals; the second includes the dietary regulations and various other topics; the third row is concerned with the relations between the sexes; the fourth is devoted to the civil and criminal law. Jacob's general approach is similar to that of Maimonides, although he lacks his interest in philosophical questions. Unlike Maimonides, however, he mentions various conflicting opinions before offering his own conclusion, which often concurs with that of his father, Asher ben Yehiel, who was himself the author of an important halakhic code.

Jacob ben Asher's really lasting contribution was his fourfold classification of the Halakhah, since it was adopted in the sixteenth century by Joseph Caro in his *Shulhan Arukh* or 'Laid Table', which has remained the most widely consulted halakhic code to this day. Caro, who had settled in Safed in Galilee after the expulsion from Spain, began by compiling an extensive critical commentary on the *Arbaah Turim*, in which he attempted to synthesize the existing diverse traditions by following, wherever possible, the majority opinion of his three outstanding predecessors, Alfasi, Maimonides and Asher ben Yehiel. From this larger work he extracted the final decisions, which he embodied in the *Shulhan Arukh*, which is a remarkably concise and orderly reference work, making an authoritative summary of the Halakhah available to a very wide public.

The *Shulhan Arukh* was quickly disseminated through printing (it was first published in 1565), and it achieved enormous popularity, which was augmented when a Polish scholar, Moses Isserles, added notes (known as the *Mappah* or 'Tablecloth') on Ashkenazi practice to complement the work of the Sephardi Caro. The differences which had grown up between Ashkenazi and Sephardi practice are a reminder that in the Middle Ages Halakhah was still open to development, whether influenced from above, by authoritative interpreters, or from below, by popular custom. Isserles was a great believer in the validity of custom, and he criticized Caro for undervaluing it. In fact many practices which have become part of the fabric of Judaism originated in the Middle Ages. They include the festivities of *Simhat Torah*, the practices associated with becoming *bar mitzvah*, and the custom of covering the head during prayer, as well as the commemoration of the dead by special prayers on the anniversary of their death each year and in the synagogue worship of the three pilgrim festivals. Through the halakhic literature and especially the codes such customs gradually acquired the force of law, and their observance was spread far beyond the locality where they were first adopted.

The *Shulhan Arukh* was the last great codification of Halakhah. Although it has given rise to numerous commentaries it has never been supplanted. Why the tradition of codification should have come to an end in this way is not clear, particularly since so much has changed in the intervening period that it is now palpably out of date. Perhaps its very success discouraged new initiative; or perhaps the accelerated rate of change made a new code seem too vast an undertaking to contemplate. Halakhic development is now embodied principally in responsa and in declarations by outstanding legal authorities and rabbinic committees. It is an unwieldy system, which demands enormous expertise and library resources, and places access to the full range of material beyond the reach of the general public and indeed of many rabbis (although this problem is currently being remedied by the use of computers). But in any case attitudes to the authority of the Halakhah and its place in Jewish life have undergone fundamental changes in the modern period.

For medieval Jews the Halakhah was divinely ordained and essentially unchanging, being revealed by God at Sinai once and for all time. There were even philosophers who argued that it would continue in force in the coming age. This was a disputed point, but all Jews agreed, against the Christians and Muslims, that God had never given and would never give any new revelation to supersede the Torah. As Maimonides put it in his celebrated Thirteen Principles of Judaism: 'This Torah of Moses will not be abrogated, nor will another Torah come from God. Nothing may be added to it or removed from it, either from the written text or from the oral commentary.' The total number of the commandments of the Torah was agreed to be 613, made up of 248 positive commandments and 365 prohibitions. (These figures are said to correspond to the number, respectively, of bones and muscles in the human body.) Although there was a certain amount of discussion of the reasons behind the various commandments, there was no real questioning of the obligation to observe them. A good life was a life lived in obedience to God's will, and God's will was completely set out in the Halakhah. The rule of Halakhah was upheld by the rabbis, who exercised far-reaching jurisdiction under the system of judicial autonomy enjoyed by the Jews in the Middle Ages. They wielded powerful sanctions, including the ultimate sanction of exclusion from the community.

All this changed in the early modern period with political emancipation and the spread of the ideas of the Enlightenment. Emancipation swept away Jewish judicial autonomy, except in certain limited areas of personal status. The rest of the Halakhah has, for practical purposes, fallen outside the scope of the courts. Even marriage is, in most countries, subject in the first instance to the civil law of the land. As for sanctions, the courts have lost most of the powers they formerly enjoyed, and they cannot even compel Jews to appear before them. Jews may still apply to the rabbinic court for a ruling on a religious question or for arbitration in a civil case, but this is now a matter of voluntary choice, and Jews commonly take their suits to civil courts. The Jewish public no longer regards rabbis as primarily lawyers, and indeed many rabbis nowadays do not see themselves as lawyers at all. A last relic of the medieval role of the rabbinate, so far as the public is concerned, is its role in supervising and certifying kosher (ritually fit) food and wine.

Meanwhile modern religious philosophy and the science of biblical criticism have undermined the supernatural basis of the Halakhah. It is now possible for Jews to ask not only *why* God ordained certain commandments but *whether* he did. Objections have been raised, on rational and moral grounds, to some of the commandments, and it has been objected that some of them are not merely anachronistic but downright unjust.

Traditional Halakhah, for example, recognizes a class of person known as *mamzer*. This is the offspring of certain categories of forbidden union, such as an incestuous or adulterous union. A *mamzer* is severely limited in his choice of marriage partner: according to the Mishnah he may only marry another *mamzer*, a proselyte, or a freed slave. Liberally-minded Orthodox authorities have tried to alleviate the problem by turning a blind eye to it, but they have not been able to abolish the category of *mamzer* or to mitigate its consequences. Another difficult problem is that of the *agunah*, a woman whose husband has disappeared. In the Halakhah there is no presumption of death, and so the *agunah* is unable to remarry. The rabbis long ago relaxed the normally strict rules of evidence so as to facilitate the recording of a husband's death and so release his widow, but where there is no evidence at all of his death the wife is tied for life. These problems, and others like them, illustrate a particular difficulty in the operation of the Halakhah. A law can only be rescinded, it was long ago decided, by a rabbinic assembly which is superior to that which decreed it. Since no contemporary assembly is deemed superior to the great Sanhedrins of ancient times, no remedy seems to be available. Thus in cases such as those just cited, where the Halakhah itself, even in its most liberal interpretation, provides no remedy, it would seem that nothing can be done by modern Orthodox authorities, short perhaps of convening a sort of ecumenical synod to undertake the reform of the law.

Reform Judaism has adopted a completely different approach to Halakhah. The early theorists of Reform were united in their conviction of the need to reform the Halakhah, even if they were divided over the extent of the required changes or the appropriate theoretical justification for reform. Samuel Holdheim (1806–60), one of the leading early Reform rabbis, insisted that even the recognition of the divine origin of the law was no obstacle to its reform: 'The present age requires the clear enunciation of the principle that a law, even though divine, prevails only so long as the situations and conditions for which it was framed continue to exist: when these change the law too must be abrogated, even if its author is God.' His contemporary Abraham Geiger advocated a thorough study of the tradition, with a view to deciding 'which rules of life are necessary, which institutions and religious practices may serve to improve the quality of religious life, which ones are moribund, and which are so at odds with our needs and circumstances as to offer no further helpful influence'.

These champions of Reform argued on the basis of a critical study of the tradition that the dogma of the immutability of the law was itself at odds with the views of the early rabbis, who themselves recognized the principle of development and change. They acknowledged no inherent distinction between laws on grounds of antiquity or sanctity; their sole concern was to refashion a Jewish practice which would be in keeping with the spirit of the age and enhance the quality of religious life, which in their day they regarded as deplorable. There was no limit, therefore, to the reforms they were prepared to countenance. Geiger, for example, while recognizing that circumcision is 'a time-honoured practice', attacks it as 'a barbaric, gory rite', and he describes the dietary regulations as 'devoid of rationale and at the same time a hindrance to the development of social relationships'.

A rather different approach was adopted by other reformers at the same time, which provoked from their Orthodox opponents the accusation of 'neo-Karaism'. David Marks, preaching at the consecration of the Reform synagogue in London in 1842, spoke as follows:

We must, as our convictions urge us, solemnly deny that a belief in the divinity of the traditions written in the Mishnah and the Jerusalem and Babylonian Talmuds is of equal obligation to the Israelite with the faith in the divinity of the Law of Moses. We know that these books are human compositions; and though we are prepared to accept with reverence from our post-biblical ancestors advice and instruction, we cannot unconditionally accept their laws. For Israelites there is but one immutable law, the sacred volume of the scriptures, commanded by God to be written down for the unerring guidance of his people until the end of time.

That this doctrine bears a close resemblance to the basic tenet of Karaism can hardly be denied. It may be questioned, however, whether this strong reassertion of the belief in the divine and eternal authority of scripture represented a sincere conviction. The neo-Karaite position, at least in such a clearly-defined form, did not long survive the growth of modern biblical criticism, even if in a vaguer form it still commands a certain sentimental assent today.

The approach initiated by Holdheim and Geiger found a willing response, and in America it was enshrined in the 'Pittsburgh Platform', adopted by a rabbinical conference convened under the powerful influence of the radical theologian Kaufmann Kohler. Here there is no distinction between Mosaic and rabbinic laws, but there is a distinction between different types of law—moral, ceremonial, and (by implication) civil and criminal. The rabbis declared:

We recognize in the Mosaic legislation a system of training the Jewish people for its mission during its national life in Palestine, and to-day we accept as binding only the moral laws and maintain only such ceremonies as elevate and sanctify our lives, but reject all such as are not adapted to the views and habits of modern civilization.

We hold that all such Mosaic and Rabbinical laws as regulate diet, priestly purity and dress originated in ages and under the influence of ideas altogether foreign to our present mental and spiritual state. They fail to impress the modern Jew with a spirit of priestly holiness; their observance in our days is apt rather to obstruct than to further modern spiritual elevation.

This formulation may appear rather negative. The 'Columbus Platform' of 1937 couched the same ideas in a more positive form (see above, page 32). An even greater sense of dissatisfaction with the negative approach of the founders may be discerned in the latest comprehensive declaration of the [Reform] Central Conference of American Rabbis, the Centenary Perspective adopted in 1976:

Judaism emphasizes action rather than creed as the primary expression of religious life, the means by which we strive to achieve universal justice and peace. Reform Judaism shares this emphasis on duty and obligation. Our founders stressed that the Jew's ethical responsibilities, personal and social, are enjoined by God. The past century has taught us that the claims made upon us may begin with our ethical obligations but they extend to many other aspects of Jewish living, including: creating a Jewish home centered on family devotion; lifelong study; private prayer and public worship; daily religious observance; keeping the Sabbath and the holy days; celebrating the major events of life; involvement with the synagogues and community; and other activities which promote the survival of the Jewish people and enhance its existence. Within each area of Jewish observance Reform Jews are called upon to confront the claims of Jewish tradition, however differently perceived, and to exercise their individual autonomy, choosing and creating on the basis of commitment and knowledge.

This formulation, and especially its concluding sentence, represents a compromise between two conflicting trends in contemporary Reform, one which stresses the autonomy of the individual and another which seeks a return to some measure of discipline, even including perhaps the codification of a 'Reform Jewish Halakhah'. It would not be accurate to say that Reform has abandoned or abolished Halakhah, although it has certainly tended to put the main emphasis in Judaism elsewhere. The Central Conference of American Rabbis has always had a Responsa Committee, whose answers are all rooted in the Halakhah. Many Reform scholars have applied themselves to the study of the rabbinic tradition, and one of them, Solomon Freehof, has published several volumes of Reform responsa (which he describes as 'not directive, but advisory'). Nevertheless it must be said that the theoretical basis of Halakhah in Reform Judaism appears somewhat nebulous.

Conservative Judaism has tried to combine the stronger features of both the Orthodox and the Reform approach while avoiding their respective shortcomings. Solomon Schechter (1848–1915), who laid much of the theological basis of the

movement, inherited the critical approach to tradition which had
become typical of European modernism. He insisted on the
diversity which had characterized the medieval tradition, and in
particular he stressed the geographical factor, that is the difference in approach which can be discerned between, for example,
the Ashkenazi and Sephardi traditions. For Schechter and those
who came after him the tradition has a strong presumptive
authority, but it does not have the last word. Louis Jacobs, the
acknowledged leader of the nascent British Conservative movement, has written:

. . . certain spiritual goods or values have become enshrined in Halakhic
institutions, irrespective of their origins, and it is these which give the
Halakhah its validity today. In this way the concept of *mitzvah* as divine
command, giving Halakhah its spiritual power, can still be preserved
even in a non-fundamentalist approach. But it surely follows that where
the Halakhah, as it has developed, either does not promote such goods
or is opposed to them, its claim on our allegiance is considerably weak-
ened. It may then have to be relinquished entirely in loyalty to the good
as taught by Judaism itself.

We may observe that the Conservative approach shares many
of the basic assumptions of Reform Judaism concerning the
nature of tradition and the response to it demanded of the
modern Jew. In particular, both absolutely reject a fundamentalist approach to the study of Bible and Talmud. On the other
hand, Conservatism allots a more central role to Halakhah
within Jewish life than does Reform, it tends to ascribe greater
force to tradition, and it rejects the Reform emphasis on the
moral as opposed to the ceremonial elements of the tradition. It
must be added, however, that Conservative Judaism embraces a
great variety of attitudes and practices, and has been reluctant to
set forth a systematic formulation of its standpoint in relation to
tradition and change. In practice it has tended towards a liberal
Orthodox approach to the Halakhah, sanctioning lenient interpretations of the existing law but fighting shy of adopting radical
solutions to the most difficult problems. In 1948, for example,
the Conservative Rabbinical Assembly held a Conference on
Jewish Law directed particularly to the problem of the *agunah*.
Its conclusion was that, in the absence of a synod with sufficient
authority to amend the law, there was little that could be done.
This view corresponds precisely to the Orthodox position outlined

above. The Assembly does, however, maintain a Committee on Jewish Law and Standards which has ratified some minor innovations.

A more explicit and consistent theory of the place and function of Halakhah in modern Judaism is to be found in Reconstructionism, which originated as an offshoot of Conservatism. The founder of Reconstructionism, Mordecai Kaplan (1881–1983), elaborated a philosophy which combines a naturalistic theology (which has no place for the commandments having been divinely revealed in the traditional sense) with a strong insistence on the life of the Jewish people, describing Judaism as a civilization rather than a religion. The religious practices of Judaism are termed 'folkways', which roughly corresponds to the traditional idea of custom (*minhag*). But whereas *minhag* occupies only a limited, if important, position in traditional Halakhah, in Kaplan's thought all Halakhah seems to acquire the status of custom. Tradition only has value to the extent that it contributes to and enhances the actual life of Jews, whether individually or as a people. Over a very long career Kaplan evolved from advocating the retention of traditional observances but reinterpreting them in the light of new ideas to propounding the need to select 'from the Judaism of the past those beliefs and practices which, either in their original or in a reinterpreted form, are compatible with what we now recognize to be authentic'. Kaplan is in favour of rejecting some 'folkways' and introducing new ones, 'calculated to render Jewish life interesting and contentful'. The connection between folkways and tradition is thus liable to become an accidental one. Moreover, Reconstructionism is open to the danger of individualism. The Reconstructionist *Guide to Jewish Ritual* recognizes a possible tension between the individual and the community, and states that 'the circumstances of life are so different for different Jews . . . that it is unreasonable to expect all of them to evaluate the same rituals in the same way'.

This danger of individualism has to be faced by all the non-Orthodox movements, which emphasize subjective criteria for religious practice. The rise of modern psychology and existentialist philosophy have tended to strengthen the claims of the individual. In the Middle Ages the closed nature of Jewish society and the belief in normative tradition combined to preserve the unified framework of Jewish life. In modern times these constraints no longer operate, and one of the most challenging questions which have to be faced is how much scope is to be allowed to the individual, or to small minorities, in claiming to lead a 'Jewish' life while rejecting traditional beliefs and practices.

The different approaches we have been considering can be examined more closely in relation to specific areas of Halakhah. The two areas which have a most direct bearing on the life of most Jews are the dietary regulations (*kashrut*) and Sabbath observance. Although these areas of Halakhah are widely regarded as constituting, as it were, the backbone of traditional Jewish life, studies conducted in America and elsewhere have revealed that the actual standards of observance, among adherents of all the various modernist movements, are not particularly high, and that they are continuing to decline. What we are concerned with here, however, is not the actual practice but the theoretical approach of each movement, and we shall consider primarily the American situation, since besides being the largest Jewish community in the world American Jewry is also the best documented and most articulate. In other countries the situation is essentially similar, but the lines may be less clearly drawn.

To begin, then, with *kashrut*, for Orthodoxy the traditional Halakhah is binding. What food one may eat is governed by a plethora of regulations deriving from the Bible and from rabbinic elaborations of the biblical rules. In the first place the Bible permits certain animals to be eaten and forbids others. Pigs, for example, are forbidden, and so are all animals which do not have a cloven hoof. Fish which do not have fins and scales are forbidden, and so are various kinds of birds, as well as creatures which 'creep on the ground'. The post-biblical tradition displays some disagreement about the details of classification, and there are some local traditions which permit species forbidden elsewhere. But in general there is clear agreement about which animals may be eaten. Even permitted animals, however, may be eaten only if they were whole and healthy, and if they have been killed and prepared in a certain way. Furthermore, on the basis of a thrice-repeated biblical prohibition on boiling a kid in its mother's milk, rabbinic law forbids meat and milk products to be cooked or eaten together, and scrupulous Orthodox Jews will go so far as to keep separate kitchen equipment and tableware for meat and milk foods. There are also some restrictions on vegetable produce, and on certain foods prepared or even handled by non-Jews. And during the festival of Passover there are special, even more restrictive, dietary rules, based for the most part on biblical regulations. In theory all these regulations are equally binding and essential, although there is some scope for liberal Orthodox authorities to take advantage of permissive interpretations by medieval halakhists in a few areas, such as the consumption of foods prepared by non-Jews.

In sharp contrast, the classical Reformers, as we have already seen, rejected all the dietary regulations as being outdated, at odds with the spirit of true religiosity, and harmful to good relations between Jews and non-Jews. In practice many Reform Jews do keep at least some of the traditional rules (just as many Orthodox Jews ignore some of them), but there is no rationale for this: it is purely a matter of personal preference. Leading Reform teachers tend either to ignore the dietary rules as not being central to their concerns or to stress that they can easily become an impediment to true religious feeling.

Conservative Judaism, in this as in so much else, occupies an intermediate position, rejecting alike the adherence to traditional norms which is characteristic of Orthodox and the radicalism of Reform. In theory there is nothing to prevent the Conservative Jew from testing each of the regulations in relation to his or her own life, to see whether it enhances or detracts from a meaningful religious existence. The result may well be a thoroughgoing adherence to the traditional Halakhah, but it may equally be a more selective approach, in which some rules (for example the prohibition on eating the flesh of certain animals) may be felt to be more important than others (for example the rigid separation of milk and meat products or the restrictions on food prepared by gentiles).

The Reconstructionist, on the other hand, is likely to be swayed primarily by the important place which the dietary laws have always occupied in the corporate life of the Jewish people. Not that he will automatically on this account maintain the totality of the regulations, but he may well feel inclined to subordinate his personal preferences to the idea of 'Jewish civilization'.

When we turn to the area of Sabbath observance, we find the same wide range of theory and of practice. The Bible singles out the seventh day as a day of rest from all work, and the later Halakhah enumerates various categories of work which is forbidden on this day. Thirty-nine such categories are listed in the Mishnah, and each category has various sub-categories. The prohibitions extend not only to the various kinds of manual work and trade, but also to travel and to the lighting of fire. Like the dietary regulations, the rules of Sabbath observance have always been considered among the most important features of the distinctively Jewish way of life. Besides the negative rules about work, there is also a positive teaching that the Sabbath should be a day of joy, traditionally expressed in various forms of physical self-indulgence as well as the avoidance of fasting and mourning.

Orthodox Judaism maintains the full rigour of the traditional Halakhah, and insofar as new questions are posed it tends to respond strictly so as to avoid any risk of infringing the prohibition on work. For example the use of electricity has been subsumed under the heading of fire, and so one may not switch on an electric light manually. On the other hand, in keeping with a constructive approach to the application of technological progress to halakhic questions, the use of time switches and other automatic devices is permitted, and considerable ingenuity is currently being devoted to developing similar ways of avoiding infringing the prohibitions. The Orthodox Sabbath is not only a 'day off work', it is a period of time out of time, a period which is hedged around with minute regulations which exclude not only cooking and most other household chores but even many recreational activities. Driving is ruled out, for example; so is gardening, playing musical instruments, and anything involving the use of money.

Reform Judaism, no less than Orthodoxy, lays stress on the observance of the Sabbath as a day set apart from other days (as we have seen, keeping the Sabbath was singled out for specific mention in the 1976 Centenary Perspective). In accordance with its guiding principles, however, it has abandoned the detailed traditional prohibitions. It is ultimately up to the individual Reform Jew to decide how he or she should celebrate the Sabbath.

Conservative Judaism, committed to the principle of revitalizing the Halakhah in keeping with the demands of the times, has tended to focus attention on positive practices associated with Sabbath observance (lighting candles on Sabbath eve, serving special Sabbath meals, attending synagogue services) rather than on the various prohibitions. It has also consciously cultivated the traditional idea of 'beautification of the commandment', in this case by promoting a warm and pleasant Sabbath atmosphere in the home and encouraging the use of attractive equipment (candlesticks, wine-cups, bread covers and so on). All this can be said to be in line with traditional Judaism. The specific relaxation of the prohibitions has been a subject of some controversy, and it has proved hard to reach agreement on definitive changes in the Halakhah. The Law Committee of the Rabbinical Assembly has, however, sanctioned the use of electricity and, more radically, it has also permitted travel on the Sabbath for the specific purpose of attending services.

The Reconstructionist *Guide to Jewish Ritual* stresses that the ultimate criterion for observance is the self-fulfilment of the individual. Thus work permitted on the Sabbath includes activity 'which the individual is unable to engage in during the week, and which constitutes not a means to making a living but a way of enjoying life'. The *Guide* proceeds, however, to permit even work connected with one's career since 'observance should not involve the frustration of a legitimate and deeply felt ambition'; it adds that 'our will to live most happily and effectively must supersede the observance of the Sabbath'.

This brief glimpse of the different approaches of the various modernist movements in American Judaism reveals, of course, a great deal of diversity, not only as regards the detailed observances but in attitudes to the legal tradition as a whole and its continuing value. The differences could be summarized as follows, always remembering that the theoretical statements are produced against the background of a very marked departure from standards of traditional observance among ordinary members of all four movements. Orthodoxy is deeply concerned to preserve the integrity and authority of the law, which is regarded as unchanging and eternally valid. Conservatism attempts to uphold the status of the law, which it regards as historically open to change; indeed it sees flexibility as one of the strengths of traditional law. Any change, however, must be introduced cautiously and must be justified by reference to the tradition itself or to certain essential and definable principles. For Reconstructionism and Reform, the legal tradition takes second place behind other considerations, and it can make at best only a weak presumptive claim on modern Jews. Both movements lay greater emphasis on the fulfilment of the individual; beyond this, Reconstructionism stresses the corporate identity of the Jewish people, while for Reform what really counts is Jewish religion and ethics in the broad sense.

Finally, it must be remarked that although in America and most other countries the demands of Jewish law have been reduced necessarily to a very small area of life, and the legal authorities enjoy very few sanctions to enforce its observance, in Israel the situation is fundamentally different. The rabbinical courts are recognized by the state, and have exclusive jurisdiction in certain areas, for example in cases of marriage and divorce involving Jews. They may even apply to the civil courts for enforcement of their judgments. Moreover, the state itself recognizes Jewish law as one of the various sources of its own law, and it attempts to maintain certain standards of observance in the public domain, notably in the areas of Sabbath observance and the dietary laws.

6

The Ethical Tradition

> Once a pagan approached Shammai and said to him:
> 'You may make a proselyte of me, provided you teach
> me the whole Torah while I stand on one foot.' Shammai
> drove him away with a yardstick he was holding. Then he
> went to Hillel. Hillel said: 'Whatever is hateful to you,
> do not do to your neighbour. That is the whole Torah:
> the rest is commentary. Now go and study.'
>
> The Talmud

Even a superficial study of the Jewish religious tradition will soon
reveal what a vital and central part is played by ethical considerations in virtually every area of the tradition. The whole of
Jewish teaching, it could be said, is grounded in a passionate
concern for justice and compassion in human relations, and in a
fundamental belief not only in the perfectibility of mankind but
in the obligation for all men and women to strive to the utmost to
conduct their own lives on the highest possible ethical plane and
to contribute, as best they can, to the betterment of society as a
whole.

Of course, ethics also occupies an important place in the Greek
philosophical tradition. Where the Jewish tradition has differed
from the Greek tradition is in refusing to see man as the measure
of all things or as the final arbiter of his own destiny, and in
refusing to consider moral principles as having any independent
existence which can be investigated through the scientific study of
man and the world. Ethics, in the Jewish tradition, can only be, at
best, a branch of religion, and is entirely dependent on religion. It
is in the light of this distinction that we must understand those
teachers who have gone so far as to proclaim, with Hillel, that the
whole of Judaism is in effect an ethical system. No doubt the
influence of Greek or Greek-inspired philosophy is never far in
the background, but all such teachers would unhesitatingly repudiate the idea that ethics is something autonomous and self-
sufficient, just as they would unhesitatingly repudiate the idea

that religion is something which can be detached from the everyday lives of ordinary men and women.

Consequently when we look at the ethical tradition in Judaism, we need to think not only about the rules for leading a virtuous life and the emphasis they are given in relation to other elements in Judaism, but also about the ways in which they are related to ideas about the character of God and his relationship with man.

The foundations of the Jewish ethical tradition are firmly laid in the ancient period, and most notably in the Bible, where such virtues as honesty, fairness and compassion are repeatedly commended to those who would obey God's will. Indeed, they are mentioned as attributes of God himself, which man is enjoined to imitate: this idea of *imitatio Dei* became one of the bases of ethical reflection in later Jewish thought. The virtuous man is called in biblical Hebrew *tzaddik*, a word which is related to the idea of justice. (The abstract noun *tzedakah* is commonly used in later Hebrew to mean 'almsgiving', one of the most positive ways in which a sense of responsibility to one's fellow man can be expressed in practice.) The biblical attitude is summed up in the celebrated utterance of the prophet Micah: 'He has told you, o man, what is good, and what the Lord demands of you; only to act justly and love mercy, and to walk humbly with your God.' The themes of personal righteousness and social justice which pervade the whole Bible emerge so strongly in the prophets that they can even find expression in the denunciation of religious observance when it has degenerated into an empty formalism. The biblical writers also interpret history in moral terms, so that national success or disaster are explained as reward or punishment by God: this attitude, too, was to have important repercussions in later Jewish thought.

The rabbinic literature, no less than the Bible, is a rich treasury of moral reflection and instruction, and some of the rabbis go so far as to see the real purpose of all the regulations of the Torah as being the improvement and perfection of man. It should be pointed out that the Christian doctrine of original sin, that is the idea that man is by nature sinful and can only be saved by divine grace, has no place in Jewish tradition. Instead, the rabbis see man as a battleground between two tendencies, the 'good inclination' and the 'inclination to evil'. The rabbis were firmly opposed to dualism, and insisted that both 'inclinations' were planted in man by God, and they further argued that the 'inclination to evil' should not be viewed only in a negative light: without it human life, with all its joys and misery, would be impossible. Nevertheless, Judaism demands that man should pursue virtue by mastering, so far as possible, the inclination to evil and subordinating it to the 'good inclination'. As for the sinner, he is strongly exhorted to find his way back to God through *teshuvah*, 'returning' or repentance, which is achieved by a recognition of one's error, and a sincere resolve not to repeat it in the future.

Underlying these rabbinic ideas is a deeply-rooted belief in man's free will. Strong biblical warrant for this belief was found in God's proclamation, 'I have set before you life and death, blessing and curse: therefore choose life . . .' In the context of Greek-inspired philosophical investigation the belief in free will was to give rise to considerable difficulties when combined in the equally strong belief in divine providence, which could be interpreted to imply the predestination of men's action. Only very rarely, however, have Jewish thinkers limited the belief in man's freedom on this account. On the contrary, so central has the belief in free will been considered that some thinkers have tended towards the other extreme, of circumscribing the scope of God's providence rather than suggest that men are not fully responsible for their actions. For without this responsibility the whole basis of classical Jewish beliefs about morality would appear to be undermined. According to these beliefs, which are strongly represented in the Bible and the rabbinic literature, all good actions are rewarded and wrong actions punished. The system of rewards and punishments is a reflection of the justice of God, as indeed is all human justice.

It would be a mistake, however, to assume on the basis of the theory of rewards and punishments that the primary motive for virtuous behaviour is expectation of reward or fear of punishment. 'Do not be like servants who serve their master so as to receive a wage, but let the fear of Heaven be upon you.' The fear which is mentioned in this ancient saying is not the fear of punishment but the fear which is mentioned in the Bible as the origin of wisdom, and which is especially associated with the virtuous life. It is a fear which is akin to awe and reverence; the fear of God is not in contrast with the love of God but complementary to it. Both alike suggest an emotional relationship with God, which

finds expression in virtuous action. In rabbinic thought actions
are not right or wrong in the abstract, they derive their moral
character from their motive. 'Do all your actions for the sake of
Heaven', as one teacher puts it, and the rabbis set great store by
the biblical maxim, 'In all your ways acknowledge him and he
will direct your paths.'

In the ancient period there is very little ethical literature as such.
We have some loosely-arranged collections of practical moral
maxims, such as are found in the biblical Book of Proverbs or the
rabbinic compilation called 'The Sayings of the Fathers' (which
remains the most-studied and best-loved of all rabbinic texts);
but there is no systematic codification of the rules for a moral
life. It is only in the Middle Ages that the ethical tradition is
channelled into a literature of its own and treated as a topic in its
own right. The medieval philosophers, under the influence of
Arabic and ultimately of Greek thought, pay considerable attention to ethics. Saadya, for example, distinguishes systematically
between two sorts of commandments, the ceremonial commandments, which rely on the authority of revelation alone, and the
ethical commandments, which are rational and would be observed
even without revelation. This distinction was to take on considerable importance in subsequent religious philosophy, particularly
in the early modern period, when the idea of rational religion
came to exercise a significant influence on what was and was not
considered central and essential in Jewish tradition, and when the
validity of the purely ceremonial commandments was opened to
question in some circles. Saadya's distinction also raises the
interesting question, much discussed by medieval philosophers,
of the autonomy of ethics: is an action good because it is commanded by God, or is it commanded by God because it is good?
Implicit in his discussion is the belief, already found in the
rabbinic writings, that certain fundamental ethical principles are
binding on all mankind, Jew and non-Jew alike, as opposed to
the detailed regulations of the Halakhah, which are binding on
Jews alone. The Neoplatonist philosopher Solomon Ibn Gabirol
broke new ground in presenting an ethical system independent of
religious tradition in his book *The Improvement of the Moral
Qualities*, while Maimonides devoted an introductory section of
his great code to a systematic discussion of the rules for an ethical
life which gives considerable (some would say excessive) prominence to the Greek idea of the avoidance of excess.

In the history of the ethical tradition a special place is occupied by the otherwise little-known Spanish moral philosopher Bahya Ibn Pakuda (late eleventh century), whose *Book of Directions to the Duties of the Heart* became the classic exposition of Jewish ethical thought. The title of the work is derived from the contrast between the outward observance of the various practical commandments, the 'duties of the limbs', and the inward, spiritual 'duties of the heart'. Bahya warns against attending to the former to the neglect of the latter. 'The duties of the limbs', he writes in his introduction, 'are of no use to us unless our hearts choose to do them and our souls desire their performance.' His book is thus intended to complement the halakhic literature, and it sets out to be no less systematic. The duties of the heart are classified and expounded in turn, and the whole scheme constitutes a kind of spiritual ladder leading up to the highest rung, which is true love of God. This scheme is not original—it is derived from the works of Muslim mystics and Bahya's ideas are deeply indebted to Arab Neoplatonism—but it represents a new departure in the Jewish tradition, and the book achieved enormous popularity, being translated from Arabic into Hebrew in the twelfth century and into many other languages subsequently.

This same somewhat mystical tendency found expression in other ethical treatises, such as the *Meditation of the Sad Soul* of Abraham bar Hiyya. Not dissimilar in many ways, although deriving from a different strand in the Jewish mystical tradition, is the work of the German Hasidim in the thirteenth century, such as Judah the Hasid of Regensburg and his disciple Eleazar of Worms. Inner piety and meticulous morality with a strong ascetic tendency are the dominant characteristics of this remarkable movement, which is also associated with an unusual branch of the medieval ethical literature, the so-called 'ethical wills', in which scholars bequeathed to their children not worldly goods but moral advice. Similar testaments are known from antiquity; in the Middle Ages they constitute a distinctive tradition, and the will of Eleazar of Worms is a notable early example.

The medieval tradition, in its most extreme form, was sometimes liable to overstep the bounds of mainstream Judaism in its devotion to asceticism, inwardness, and rigorous personal purity. In general, however, Judaism has always turned its back on inward-looking pietism, and insisted that Jewish life is to be lived in the family and the wider community. It has eschewed asceticism, and favoured if anything a moderate self-indulgence, on the grounds that the pleasures of this world are also among the gifts of God. It is in this broader context that morality takes its place, within the framework of the Halakhah, to maintain the fabric of Jewish society and give expression to the Torah as God's will for all mankind. The attributes of saintliness are admired, but with severe reservations, and their attainment may not be within the reach of most ordinary mortals. The purpose of morality, according to this common view, is less to effect the perfection of the individual than to prevent the debasement of society.

In the nineteenth century the Lithuanian Musar movement, founded by Israel Salanter (1810–83), represents a remarkable renewal of the medieval spiritual and ethical tradition, from which it takes its name (*musar* being the Hebrew for 'ethics'). Unlike Polish Hasidism, with which it has some features in common and of which it was in some sense a rival, the Musar movement did not discourage the academic study of the Talmud, but urged that it should be complemented by deep personal piety and by meditation on ethical texts, many of which were revived and republished as a result of this renewed interest. Study of these texts was a feature of the 'Musar houses' where both professional scholars and members of the wider public would retire for a period of self-scrutiny every day, and in the academies which came under the influence of the movement they were chanted aloud to special tunes.

Meanwhile in western Europe the Enlightenment brought about a revival of interest in the philosophical discussion of the place of ethics in Judaism. The description of Judaism as 'ethical monotheism', which became commonplace in the later nineteenth century, served the double purpose of underlining the affinity of Judaism with the 'religion of reason' while stressing the ethical values which (insofar as they derive from the Bible) Judaism shares with Christianity. Such arguments served a useful apologetic purpose in their day, bolstering the respectability of Judaism in the eyes of rationalists and Christians alike. Thus the Enlightenment, while it challenged so much else in Judaism, actually had the effect of reinforcing the ethical tradition as being the most rational and universal ingredient in the Jewish tradition.

For the nineteenth-century Jewish philosophers there was no argument about the nature of Jewish ethics or its importance in Judaism: the only problem was how to accommodate it within a particularistic religion.

The nineteenth-century reformers, with their radical critique of the Halakhah, eagerly promoted the idea of 'Prophetic Judaism', and what they had in mind was not only the universal vision of the biblical prophets but also their appeal to moral values in challenging established power and practice and their championing of deprived and underprivileged members of society. It was only natural that they should stress the distinction between ceremonial and ethical commandments, and endorse the latter to the detriment of the former. Nor were they alone. Jewish secularists, and especially the socialists among them, also laid emphasis on the moral values which Judaism had given the world, and they too were inclined to recall the universalism of the prophets as an antidote to the particularism which they felt to be a bane of Jewish existence.

The major difference between reformers and secularists lay, of course, in their attitude to religion. Reform Judaism remains within the paths mapped out by Jewish tradition in linking love of man with love of God, while secular Judaism is closer to the Greek ideal in placing human needs at the centre. Nevertheless, when it comes to a programme of action there is little difference between the two. The section on ethics in the Columbus Platform of 1937 encapsulates the Reform position. The first paragraph is a fair summary of traditional Jewish teachings, while the second, still entirely consonant with that tradition, could be accepted in its entirety by most secularists:

Ethics and Religion. In Judaism religion and morality blend into one indissoluble unity. Seeking God means to strive after holiness, righteousness and goodness. The love of God is incomplete without the love of one's fellowmen. Judaism emphasizes the kinship of the human race, the sanctity and worth of human life and personality and the right of the individual to freedom and the pursuit of his chosen vocation. Justice to all, irrespective of race, sect or class, is the inalienable right and the inescapable obligation of all. The state and organized government exist in order to further these ends.

Social Justice. Judaism seeks the attainment of a just society by the application of its teachings to the economic order, to industry and commerce, and to national and international affairs. It aims at the elimination of man-made misery and suffering, of poverty and degradation, of tyranny and slavery, of social inequality and prejudice, of ill-will and strife. It advocates the promotion of harmonious relations between warring classes on the basis of equity and justice, and the creation of conditions under which human personality may flourish. It pleads for the safeguarding of childhood against exploitation. It champions the cause of all who work and of their right to an adequate standard of living, as prior to the riches of property. Judaism emphasizes the duty of charity, and strives for a social order which will protect men against the material disabilities of old age, sickness and unemployment.

While no one would quarrel with the content of this interpretation of traditional Jewish ethical teaching, the more conservative trends would insist on the link between ethics and Halakhah in its widest sense. In fact recent studies of contemporary ethical problems in such areas as sexual relations, business, and medicine have demonstrated how rich the halakhic tradition is in moral insights which can still be applied fruitfully in today's very different situations. The results of such investigations, needless to say, are not always congruent with the most advanced views of western secular thinkers, and liberal Jewish critics have pointed to certain traditional attitudes which they feel are no longer appropriate or helpful; but in general they reveal a compassionate concern for the rights of the individual, and particularly the victim of exploitation and oppression, balanced by a view of the welfare of society as a whole, which is well within the broad trends of modern thinking, and which can make a genuine contribution to serious contemporary discussion.

7

The Mystical Tradition

Songs I weave and tunes I utter, for my soul doth pant
for thee,
Longing in thy powerful shade to know thy secret
mystery.
As thy glory I describe, my mind suspires to soar above,
So I sing about thy glory, glorifying thy name with love.

All unseeing I sing thy glory, all unknowing I speak of
thee
By thy faithful prophets showing images of mystery.
Calling on thy works they named thee, picturing thy
power and might;
Drawing on thy deeds they framed thee, who wert hidden
from their sight.
Every vision paints its picture, but in essence thou art
One,
Full of years or youthful victor, flushed with pride of
battles won . . .

From the 'Hymn of Glory'

The 'Hymn of Glory' is a medieval composition which still has an
honoured place in the Ashkenazi liturgy. In many congregations
it is sung before the open ark at the end of the Additional Service
every Sabbath, the singing often being led (inappropriate as it
may seem) by a young child. The hymn is one of the most concentrated and enduring expressions of the mystical tendency in
Judaism. It is mystical in two distinct senses. In the first place it
dwells on the essential unknowability of God, the hidden essence
of which all the epithets are only approximate images. But it also
expresses the urgent personal longing for intimacy with the
Divine which is the perennial hallmark of the mystic. Yet for all
the mystical language and emotional urgency of the poem, there
is something about it which may make us question whether its
mysticism is identical with mysticism as the term is commonly
used. We tend to think of the mystic as withdrawing into himself,

communing with God in utter privacy, despising communal experience and public religion. Although there have been Jewish mystics of this type, it is hard for the Jew to cut himself off from the outward forms of Judaism. Some of the most celebrated Jewish mystics of all time are also remembered for more conventional achievements, in the realm of law, philosophy or traditional biblical commentary. There is an interesting tension here, which can be sensed also in the words of the hymn. The poet, while admitting that God's essence is unknowable, seeks images of him in the words of the Bible, as interpreted by the rabbis. Thus the images of the old man and the youthful warrior, representing two contrasting pictures of God, are drawn respectively from the Book of Daniel and from the Song of Songs, which is interpreted by the rabbis as an allegory of the love between God and Israel. There is something quintessentially Jewish in this linking of mystical yearning with the experience and destiny of the whole people. This characteristic feature of Jewish mysticism makes it hard to isolate the mystical tradition in Judaism: the mystical elements tend to be intimately entwined in the tradition as a whole.

After all, it was taken for granted until relatively recently that the whole of Judaism was rooted in a kind of mystical encounter with God. In the Bible God speaks perfectly naturally to the patriarchs and prophets, and the roots of Jewish mysticism can be traced to their visions and passions. We have seen that as late as the 1850s so modern (and unmystical) a thinker as Samson Raphael Hirsch could proclaim that 'For Orthodox Judaism . . . "God spoke to Moses" is a simple supernatural fact just as one man speaks to another.' Yet there is a distinction to be drawn between revelation and mystical experience: in revelation God breaks through, as it were, into the human domain to impart some knowledge of himself and his will, whereas the mystic is a human being straining to penetrate the divine domain. The experience of the mystic is an emotional experience which has no precise form or content, and when he looks for words in which to communicate his experience he tends to turn to received tradition. It is this which gives Jewish mysticism its distinctive flavour. Although the experience of the mystic is sublimely personal, it tends to become clothed in traditional forms. This saves the Jewish mystic from complete individualism, which is so foreign to Judaism, and compels him to integrate his ideas, at least up to a point, within the wider currents of Jewish tradition.

Since this tradition is very largely a scholarly tradition, grounded in the sacred scriptures and their interpretation, Jewish mysticism has often taken the form, at least outwardly, of biblical exposition. It appears that in antiquity there were two distinct schools of mystical investigation devoted respectively to the biblical account of the creation of the world and to Ezekiel's vision of the divine throne-chariot. In the Middle Ages the great classic of the Kabbalah, the Zohar, essentially takes the form of a midrash on the Torah. Of course the mystical interpretation is different from more conventional commentary, not only in its content but also in its presuppositions. The mystics sometimes liken the Torah to a living being, the literal meaning of the words corresponding to the body while the hidden mysteries correspond to the soul. There is a curious medieval idea that the whole Torah can be read, by one who has eyes to see it, not as narratives and commandments, but as a sequence of names of God. Here we see the mystical approach to tradition at its most extreme, but this attitude is perhaps not so very far removed from one of the dominant trends in conventional rabbinic exegesis, which sees every letter of the Torah, every jot and tittle, as a clue to some hidden mystery. And the rabbinic interpretation of the Song of Songs as an allegory of the love-relationship between God and Israel prepares the ground for a good deal of later mystical imagery, such as we find in the 'Hymn of Glory'.

The 'Hymn of Glory' originated in the circles of the German Hasidim or *Hasidei Ashkenaz*, and its author is commonly thought to be Judah the Hasid (d.1217), one of the leading members of the movement. As we have seen, the German Hasidim carried to an extreme which is hard to parallel in the Jewish tradition the pursuit of asceticism, ritual, and ethical rigour, and they combined it with a passionate interest in mystical theology, religious symbolism and even magic. In many ways these concerns have more in common with Christian spirituality than with mainstream Judaism, and it has been plausibly argued that they were directly influenced by contemporary Christian ideas and practices. Most of them, however, have clear antecedents in certain Jewish circles in Gaonic Babylonia, and some of them can be traced back to Palestinian Judaism in the Graeco-Roman period.

This is particularly true of the so-called *Merkavah* mysticism, the contemplation of the mystery of God's heavenly chariot-throne, often associated with ascetic practices, magical rituals, hymns and incantations, and secretly-transmitted knowledge. Elements of this quest for a mystical encounter with the Divine have been found in the ancient apocalyptic writings (such as the Book of Enoch) and the Dead Sea Scrolls, and also in early Rabbinic Judaism, where, although treated with great circumspection, it is associated with the names of leading rabbis. It appears to have emerged in Palestine under Greek influence, and it exercised an important influence in its turn on early Christianity, on Christian and pagan Gnosticism, and on Rabbinic Judaism in Babylonia. The key term *kavod*, 'Glory', can be traced back to the earliest strands in this esoteric tradition. It is used as a name of God in the context of mystical speculation, and it can even be used to denote this type of speculation itself. Saadya introduced the term into his philosophical discussion of the unity of God. Stressing God's absolute unity and incorporeality, he insisted that the anthropomorphism of the Bible (that is, the description of God's activity in terms drawn from the human body) is purely metaphorical. As for the prophetic visions of God, Saadya argued that the prophets did not see God himself, but only his Glory, which was itself created by God. This theory of the 'created Glory' was to become an important part of the theology of the German Hasidim. It allowed them to use intensely physical language in talking about the 'Glory', while maintaining the utter incorporeality of the hidden 'Creator'.

How did these eastern ideas come to penetrate the thought of German Jewry? They probably travelled with Talmudic rabbinism itself, reaching Germany by way of France and Italy. The German Hasidim themselves claimed that some of the Babylonian elaborations of *Merkavah* mysticism were communicated in Italy by a ninth-century wonderworking mystic named Abu Aaron of Baghdad to Moses ben Kalonymos, who later settled in Germany and became the ancestor of many of the leaders of the German pietistic movement, including Eleazar of Worms. In fact there is some evidence that *Merkavah* mysticism was already established in Italy and France before the time of Abu Aaron, but he may well have been responsible (together perhaps with other travelling magicians) for introducing some newer Babylonian ideas into the west, such as the use of numerology (*gematria*) to establish links between the magical names of God and the words of the Bible and the liturgy. Saadya's interpretation of the Glory was spread through Hebrew translations and paraphrases of his works, while Neoplatonist philosophical ideas, which also influenced the Hasidim, were probably transmitted by wandering Spanish teachers, such as Abraham Ibn Ezra, who travelled to France and even to England in the middle of the twelfth century.

In speaking of a mystical tradition we are thus really speaking about a number of different, interwoven strands, which surface and combine in different ways at different times. At the same time as Judah the Hasid and the other Hasidim were developing their ideas in Germany, a different school of mystical speculation was emerging in Provence, where the *Sefer ha-Bahir* was edited, on the basis of texts coming from the east or perhaps also from Germany, in the second half of the twelfth century. This work combines *Merkavah* mysticism with plainly Gnostic symbolism and with traditional elaborations of biblical stories to lay the basis for the theosophical speculation which was to be developed into the Spanish Kabbalah. Meanwhile the Islamic mysticism of the sufis was feeding other streams of Jewish mysticism, notably through the *Duties of the Heart* of Bahya Ibn Pakuda: this manual of instruction for the Hasid who aspires to communion with God achieved considerable success, even among Kabbalists. The influence of sufism is also felt strongly in Egypt, where the title 'Hasid' was applied to a number of rabbis who adopted the path of introspection and self-discipline, and where the son and grandson of Maimonides composed sufi works and attracted a certain following.

The three main elements within the mystical tradition are knowledge of God, love of God, and communion or reunion with God. The knowledge of God tends to take the form among mystics of esoteric knowledge or *gnosis* which is transmitted from teacher to pupil and generally guarded from dissemination among the public at large. Whereas the Muslim sufis generally traced their mystical knowledge back to Muhammad, the origin of the Jewish esoteric tradition was sometimes associated with figures in the very remote past, such as Abraham or even Adam, with the implication that it is independent of the revelation at Sinai. However it can as easily take the form of an allegorical or symbolic interpretation of the Torah, in which the Hebrew words are held to be keys to hidden truths. These esoteric interpretations were often represented as going back to the early rabbis. The mystic does not receive a new revelation, but rediscovers the meaning of Torah, which speaks with a living voice to each man who approaches it with an open heart.

The mystical knowledge of God is also fed, as we have already seen, by external sources, in which a very significant part is played by Neoplatonist philosophy, with its insistence on the unknowability of the ultimate One, which is linked to the world by a series of emanations. Emanationism is a prominent feature of the kabbalistic system. Addressing themselves to the problem of the relationship between God and the visible world, the kabbalists agreed that God in himself is beyond all human knowledge, even beyond mystical intuition. Between this utterly perfect and unknowable being, generally called *Ein Sof* ('The Infinite'), and the created world the link is supplied by a series of emanations, beginning with the Divine Will and proceeding through a sequence of ten 'Sefirot'. The similarity of this sytem with that of the Neoplatonist philosophers is obvious, but it is also only superficial, since the kabbalistic emanations are all within the Godhead, and even the lowest and most accessible of them is still beyond the physical world. The kabbalistic system is thus properly to be called theosophical rather than philosophical. Its prolific literature bulks large in the history of Jewish exploration of the nature of God, but it is an exploration conducted far from the beaten paths of rational enquiry.

In a sense the theosophy of the Kabbalah can be seen as a reaction against the remoteness and abstraction of the God of the philosophers. But the *Via Negativa* of the philosophers, the denial of the possibility of ascribing any positive attributes to God as the biblical writings appear to do, can also be seen as opening the door to mysticism. The mystic responds to the challenge of God's unknowability not by denying it or turning his back on it, but by reaching out passionately towards it. This response can be observed even in people who are normally thought of as philosophers rather than mystics. Thus Solomon Ibn Gabirol's poetry expresses a powerful personal yearning for knowledge of God, and even Maimonides sometimes appears to describe the quest for knowledge of God in mystical terms. In fact it is not easy to draw the line between religious philosophy and mysticism, just as it is not always easy to draw the line between biblical exegesis and mystical allegory. The fascination of the German Hasidim and the Kabbalists with the idea of God's essential unknowability is attested in their efforts to safeguard it by distinguishing between the ultimate God, who is beyond all possible human knowledge, and his various powers or manifestations, which can legitimately be contemplated and explored. Of course this distinction can easily lead to dualism, or even to polytheism, and the Jewish mystics were careful to guard against any imputation of a denial of the essential unity of God.

The love of God depends on the knowledge of God, since one can only love what one knows (as has often been pointed out, the Bible uses the same verb for 'know' and 'love'). The love of God is described by the rabbis as the greatest of all the commandments. But the rabbis tend to understand this love in terms of action: love of God is expressed in obedience to the commandments. For the mystics it is a powerful emotion. Bahya defines it as 'the soul's spontaneous longing for her Creator'; but he sees this love as the final goal for which the rest of his instruction is a preparation. Only when man has perceived God's majesty and prostrated himself in fear before it will love be stirred in his heart. Maimonides has a similar argument: the simple are taught to serve God out of fear; it is only when one comes to know God that one can begin to love him. 'Where there is little knowledge there is little love; where there is much knowledge there is much love.' This thought is the basis of the mystic ideal of *devekut*, 'cleaving' to God.

Devekut is the goal of the mystic's endeavour, in which all other thoughts are driven out of his mind and he experiences nothing but the contemplation of God. The Kabbalists speak rapturously about this intimate communion, but they are generally careful not to describe it as an actual union of the soul with God, in which the individuality of the soul is dissolved.

For the Jewish mystics it was prayer that served as the main vehicle for the upward journey to the contemplation of the Divine. The Kabbalists developed a system of meditative *kavvanot* (intentions) which focused on the secret meaning of each prayer, and helped the worshipper to use the canonical words of the prayer as stepping stones towards a perception of the Names of God and the mysteries of the universe. This *kavvanah* is basically an extension of the *kavvanah* which accompanies the observance of any commandment: originally a self-conscious attention to the action itself and the reason for doing it, for the Kabbalists it became a concentration on the symbolic kabbalistic significance of the act. In the case of worship, which is less tied to specific actions, this approach soon leads to a comprehensive meditative exercise, and worship is transformed from a public to an essentially private and personal activity. The *kavvanot*, many of which were eventually formulated and incorporated in the published liturgy, were really different for each worshipper and for each moment, and it was held that no two prayers were ever alike. This was particularly stressed in the later, Lurianic Kabbalah, and Isaac Luria used to give his disciples meditative exercises based on combinations of letters in the divine name. This system of meditation on letter-combinations (*tzerufim*) derives from an earlier tradition associated particularly with the name of Abraham Abulafia (b. 1240), whose 'prophetic Kabbalah' offered various techniques to aid the ascent of the soul, such as breathing exercises and incantations. These techniques can be readily paralleled in the practice of the Christian hesychasts and the Muslim sufis, not to mention the yogis. Mysticism is the point where all religions come closest to each other, and influence from one to another is probable, even if it is also likely that some techniques developed independently along parallel lines.

Mysticism as the quest for communion with God was given an important turn in the Lurianic Kabbalah, with its doctrine of *tikkun*. *Tikkun* means 'reparation', and to understand what it means it is necessary to know something of the Lurianic theory of the origin of the world. Whereas in earlier Kabbalah everything proceeds from the *Ein Sof* in a relatively orderly and consistent process of emanation and creation, the Lurianic system introduces a number of complications and changes of course, of which the most important are conveyed through the images of *tzimtzum* ('contraction') and *shevirah* (the 'breaking of the vessels'). The idea of *tzimtzum* arises from the difficulty that the very infinity of the *Ein Sof* appears to allow no room for creation. Accordingly in the Lurianic system the very first event is a contraction of God into himself, as it were, leaving a kind of vacuum in which the world can come into being. This drastic revision of earlier theory, important though it is within the content of Kabbalah, remains in the domain of the speculative, and its main effect is to remove the taint of pantheism, which in many people's minds attached to Kabbalah, by establishing a clear division between the infinite God and the finite world. The 'breaking of the vessels' has far more practical implications. According to this theory, as the creative light of God was pouring into inchoate Creation, some of the vessels or channels containing it collapsed under the strain and broke. The fragments scattered and fell, together with the sparks of divine light trapped in them, giving birth to base matter and to the *sitra ahra*, the 'other side' which is the domain of evil. More than this, the whole well-ordered scheme of the universe was dislocated by the collapse, and nothing remained in its allotted place. The 'breaking of the vessels' is thus nothing less than a cosmic catastrophe, preceding even the creation of the world as we know it. Consequently the whole cosmos, and not just mankind or the material world, is in urgent need of salvation or reparation (*tikkun*).

This *tikkun* becomes the main concern of Lurianic Kabbalah, and an important active role in it is allotted to man himself, and specifically to the Jew, who, by a life of mystical devotion to the divine law, has it in his power to release the imprisoned sparks and so bring about the redemption not only of the world but, so to speak, of God himself. This is the significance of the spiritual exercises of the Lurianic school: their purpose is not just the blissful reunion of the individual soul with God, but the reparation of the whole cosmos. In this work God and man are bound together by a closer bond than in Talmudic Judaism or even in the earlier Kabbalah represented by the Zohar: God and man need each other, and man's actions can have an effect on God himself.

The Lurianic Kabbalah gained enormous popularity, and from the beginning of the seventeenth century it swept across the Jewish world like a forest fire, exploding in the middle of the century in the messianic upheaval which focused on the person of Shabbetai Zvi. A century later it was given a significant boost by the Polish Hasidim, who popularized its ideas and disseminated them among a wider, largely unlettered Jewish public. The Hasidim stressed the attitude of sincerity and selfless devotion

which is within the reach of all men. The intellectual contemplation of the Kabbalists was replaced by a highly charged emotional
enthusiasm which was especially manifested in prayer. The
Hasidim prayed with an intensity which aimed to detach them
from the trammels of the corporeal world and sought a complete
union with the divine nothingness. *Kavvanah* (intention),
devekut (cleaving), and *hitlahavut* (enthusiasm) are key terms in
Hasidism, and some of the Hasidic masters go so far as to seek
the complete annihilation of the self in union with the divine. A
development which is particularly associated with Shneour
Zalman of Lyady (1747–1813), the founder of the Habad school
of Hasidism, reinterprets the Lurianic doctrine of *tzimtzum* so as
to restore the essential unity of God and the world. According to
this view, only God really exists; everything else is contained
within him, and there is no place empty of him. The universe is
kept in being by the unfailing power which emanates constantly
from the *Ein Sof*; without this it would vanish in an instant. In
Habad Hasidism the stress is removed from emotion and placed
once again on intellectual contemplation. The worshipper, for
example, rather than submitting blindly to the upsurge of joyful
ecstasy within him, directs his mind to the way in which the *Ein
Sof* keeps the whole universe in being, tracing the path of the
divine light from world to world down to this material world and
back up again to the *Ein Sof*, until his heart achieves the ecstatic
union with the divine. The Hasidic yearning for personal union
with God who is all in all is typified in the famous song of Levi
Yitzhak of Berdichev:

> Wherever I go—you!
> Whatever I think—you!
> Only you, you again, always you!
> You! You! You!

The mystical tradition in its most intense forms has virtually
disappeared, killed off by the destruction and dispersal of the old
communities where it was once a vital force, in Morocco, the
Middle East, and in eastern Europe, and by the spirit of rationalism and materialism which now prevails in the main centres of
contemporary Jewry. There are some surviving communities of
Kabbalists and Hasidim, but they are few and isolated from the
main streams of Jewish life, serving more as a reminder of past

glories than as a living force in Judaism today. After a period of suspicion and outright hostility in the nineteenth century, Jewish scholarship has turned its attention to the mystical literature, and some very serious scientific studies have emerged, dominated by the pioneering work of the late Gershom Scholem. But scholarly investigation of mysticism is a very different thing from mysticism itself, and these studies only serve to underline the difference between the mystical and the scientific mind.

About the influence of the mystical tradition on modern Judaism there is very little to be said. There have been a few attempts to integrate kabbalistic or Hasidic ideas within a modern philosophy of Judaism, of which the most original is the mystical Zionism of Abraham Isaac Kook, Ashkenazi Chief Rabbi of Palestine from 1922 to 1935. The influential modern religious thinkers Martin Buber and Abraham Joshua Heschel were deeply marked by their encounter with Hasidism, and they both published a number of studies of the subject. Buber, in particular, can be credited with a remarkable renewal of interest in the potential Hasidic contribution to modern spirituality, and although it has been questioned how far his portrait of Hasidism is an accurate one he has certainly succeeded in making the spirit of Jewish mysticism speak with a living voice to people reared in the western rationalist tradition. But the enduring influence of Jewish mysticism is to be found, if anywhere, in the liturgy of the synagogue, where despite all the modern reforms the prayers of the *Merkavah* mystics, the hymns of the German Hasidim and the Kabbalists and the soulful tunes of the Polish Hasidim still live on, appealing to the hearts rather than the minds of modern worshippers, and subtly shaping their faith.

8

The Theological Tradition

Great is the living God and to be praised:
existing and unlimited by time.

Unique in his uniqueness he is One,
concealed in his infinite unity.

He has no body, no substance or form,
no image can define his holiness.

Preceding all created things, the First,
with no beginning to his primacy.

Eternal Lord is he, and all the world
declares his greatness and his majesty.

To men he chose to glorify his name
he gave abundant gifts of prophecy.

No prophet has there been in Israel
like Moses, who beheld him face to face.

Through him, the prophet 'faithful in his house',
God gave his people the one true Torah.

Nor will he ever abrogate his law
or substitute another in its place.

He sees into the secrets of our hearts
and knows the end of all things in advance.

For all good deeds he grants a due reward,
but punishes the sinner for his sin.

Finally our Anointed will he send
to save those who await the glorious end.

The dead our loving God to life will raise:
For ever be his name adored with praise!

Yigdal

That this austerely theological hymn, which is actually a versified summary of the Thirteen Principles of Maimonides, should have become and should remain one of the most popular of all the hymns of the synagogue may seem surprising to anyone who believes that Judaism has no creed and little interest in theology. But in fact there are many other equally theological hymns and prayers, and Maimonides' Thirteen Principles can still be found in many prayer books recast as a creed, each statement beginning, 'I believe with perfect faith that . . .' Yet it is also true that theology has never occupied in Judaism the central place that it has in Christianity. If Jewish authorities have occasionally anathematized or excommunicated other Jews on theological grounds, such instances have been rare indeed compared to the Christian experience, and the issues involved have generally been in the area of the binding authority of scripture or tradition, rather than more narrowly theological questions of the nature of the Godhead, which have so often given rise to drastic action in Christianity. On these latter questions Judaism has tended to display a toleration of dissent which may almost appear to border on agnosticism.

Jewish theology, like its Christian and Muslim counterparts, derives from the encounter between Semitic and Greek habits of thought, and more particularly from the application of systematic rational investigation to the image of God and his relationship to the world presented in the Bible. In the Bible God is encountered from the outset as a larger-than-life, but none the less very real, person. He is the starting point and the central thread around which the rest of the story revolves: the biblical story can be read virtually as a biography of God, at least in so far as his relationship with the world is concerned. His existence is taken for granted, not proved, and his personality is also assumed, not explored: on the contrary, it is man whose existence derives from God, and man's character is seen as a reflection of that of God. God is the one reliable certainty in the biblical world, and everything else depends on him. He creates the world out of chaos, makes man in his own image, and presides over human history like a father watching over his family or a king ruling over his people. He speaks, and man responds. Man's highest duty is to be true to the role allotted to him by God, and his ultimate destiny is entirely in God's hands.

This approach is diametrically opposed to that developed by the Greek philosophers, in which man is the measure of all things, and questions about the essential character of the world and human existence are explored on the basis of human experience using the tools provided by human reasoning. The Greek thinkers reached out gradually from mythological tales towards a perception of absolute values and principles which transcend the multifarious details of what they called the 'visible world' and help to make sense of them by suggesting an underlying unity and purpose. The result is an increasingly refined account of the workings of the universe, but one in which the ultimate realities are uncompromisingly abstract and remote from everyday experience. The Greek thinkers also tended, particularly under the influence of Plato, to exalt the invisible, 'intelligible' world at the expense of the visible world, and to characterize the latter as merely a pale and unreliable reflection of the former. True understanding of the world is therefore the exclusive prerogative of the intellectual, who alone is able to pierce through the veil of the misleading phenomena to the ultimate truth beyond.

The rationalism of the Greek thinkers, with their belief that everything in the world can be understood and explained in terms of a single system of ideas, gained remarkably widespread acceptance even at a popular level, but the formative phases in the evolution of early Judaism took place away from the main centres of Greek thought (the Alexandrian synthesis represented by Philo was a dead end as far as Judaism is concerned). The Jewish intellectual tradition was fostered in the rabbinic schools, where the main focus of study was the Bible and Halakhah. Although many of the early rabbis were perfectly at home in at least the more vulgar currents of Greek thought, they do not seem to have thought it worth their while to place the study of metaphysics high on their curriculum (or else, and there are traces of this in the literature, they felt that it was too dangerous to be expounded in the classroom, still less in a more public forum). Hence, it would appear, the lack of centrality of theological thought in classical Judaism, and the lack of a continuous theological tradition.

But even if the rabbis did not apparently attempt to set out their theology in systematic form, they did hold firmly to certain theological beliefs, which were occasionally tested against rival formulations. The fundamental belief, which they consistently insisted on and defended, was the unity of God: God is one not only in the sense that he has no partners or rivals, but also in the sense that he is unique, totally unlike any other being. The rabbis are adamant in their rejection of crude pagan polytheism and idolatry, but they also attack subtler threats to the unity of God, such as the idea that different aspects or 'powers' can be distinguished within the Godhead, or that the supreme being has an assistant, a sort of 'second God', who created the world. We can only catch snatches of these ideas in the course of fragmentary reports of theological debates, but it is clear that any conception which might pose a challenge to God's unity was met by a resolute and dogmatic affirmation of God's simple and all-encompassing oneness. In fact the rabbis were well aware that God can be perceived and described in many different ways, and that the Bible itself has different names for him. They themselves refer to him by different names, such as 'The Place', 'Heaven', 'The Creator', 'Lord of the Universe', 'The Merciful', and so forth, and in the formulation of the liturgical blessings they regularly single out specific aspects of his activity, such as 'Redeemer of Israel', 'Hearkener to Prayer', or 'Reviver of the Dead'. They also draw fruitful lessons from the many different images of God which appear in the Bible, such as Father, King, Shepherd, Judge, Redeemer, and in particular they distinguish thirteen different attributes of God in Exodus 34:6–7 'The Lord, the Lord, God, merciful and gracious, patient, and abundant in love and truth, maintaining love to thousands, forgiving iniquity, transgression and sin, and acquitting.' Nevertheless the basic doctrine of God's unity overrides all the different manifestations and images, and serves to bind them all together into a coherent whole.

Even a brief summary of the rabbinic view of God has to take account of its complexity, which is fraught with internal contrasts and even paradoxes. God is seen as transcendent, remote and unknowable, and yet he is active in the world, close to those who call on him, and knowable by experience. For the presence of God dwelling within the world the rabbis have a special name, *Shekhinah*, and they can even describe the Shekhinah as sharing in man's suffering or going into exile with the people of Israel. Again, God is seen as majestic, and ruthless in his justice, and yet he is also loving, kind and forgiving. The paradox here is self-evident; the rabbis view the divine attributes of mercy and justice as somehow holding each other in balance. Moreover, God is all-good, and demands righteousness from man, yet he allows evil to exist in his world, and grants man free will to choose between right and wrong. Then, as the creator of the world God is the God of all mankind, yet he has a special relationship with the people of Israel. This relationship is not based on any particular merit of Israel, but is a free act of grace or choice on God's part. Through his relationship with Israel, he exhibits his relationship to the world as a whole. Although God's power is revealed in the natural world, he has also revealed himself to individuals, such as the patriarchs and prophets, and above all to Moses who received at Sinai the embodiment of God's teaching and will in the Torah, which serves as a symbol of the covenant between God and Israel and makes Israel into a holy nation, that is a nation 'separated' to the service of God. Israel are God's witness in the world, and they are also his instrument in the redemption of all mankind, who will eventually be brought to abandon all false gods and recognize his supreme sovereignty.

This rabbinic theology, rooted in the unity of God and the three pillars of creation, revelation and redemption, is still highly influential in Judaism today, since it is embodied in the familiar words of the synagogue liturgy. It is also implicit in the character of the festivals of the liturgical year: thus New Year is the anniversary of the creation; *Shavuot* commemorates the revelation at Sinai; while redemption, in all its forms, is celebrated at Passover.

It was only in the Middle Ages that rigorous philosophical thought and a serious interest in metaphysical questions came to the fore in Judaism, at least in certain circles. The influence of Greek ideas is clearly visible here, mediated by Muslim scholarship. Saadya, the first really important Jewish theologian since the time of Philo, lived in Iraq at the time of the early flowering of Islamic religious philosophy; he was a contemporary of such important Muslim thinkers as al-Ash'ari and al-Farabi, and his philosophical work is conceived in the spirit of the main Islamic rationalist school, the Mu'tazilite Kalam, which pioneered the interpretation of Islamic doctrine in terms of Greek philosophical thought. From the time of Saadya on, the contours of Jewish religious philosophy are remarkably similar to those of Islamic thought. Neoplatonism reached its climax in Islam with Avicenna

(980–1037), and in Judaism with Ibn Gabirol (*c.* 1020–*c.* 1057), the thought of both men being tinged with distinctive mystical elements. The criticisms of philosophy associated in Islam with the name of al-Ghazali (1058–1111) can be paralleled in Judaism in the work of Judah ha-Levi (before 1075–1141). Even more striking is the fact that the greatest Aristotelian philosophers in both traditions, Averroes (1126–98) and Maimonides (1135–1204), were contemporaries and natives of Cordoba in Spain; both men later exercised an important influence on thirteenth-century Christian scholasticism.

The medieval philosophers saw it as their task to reconcile the theological beliefs drawn from the Bible and developed in the rabbinic tradition with the current rationalist philosophy derived ultimately from classical Greek sources. They were motivated to this task primarily by the need to defend the traditional faith against the objections of rationalist intellectuals who derided it as being insufficiently rigorous and in conflict with rational principles, and they aimed by their defence to keep such intellectuals within the Jewish fold and to allay the doubts they might raise in the minds of simpler believers. But in the process they also answered criticisms raised against Judaism by exponents of Islam and Christianity, and against rabbinic Judaism by adherents of Karaism. Thus their first purpose was apologetic. But rather than simply rejecting the philosophical approach out of hand or counterattacking by undermining its claims they entered into a real dialogue with philosophy, accepting its main premises and using the tools of reason to enrich the understanding of Judaism and achieve a consistent and systematic exposition of its beliefs. The early thinkers, of whom the greatest was Saadya, tended to follow the lead of the Mu'tazilite Kalam, expounding traditional beliefs using philosophical terminology and argumentation, and attempting to show that there was no inherent conflict between religion and reason. Very soon, however, it became clear that reason was more than simply a tool for the clarification of traditional beliefs, more even than an alternative way to the truth. For the philosopher reason is the highest of the human faculties, the most reliable guide to knowledge beyond the limited range of the senses. Even Saadya, although he maintains firmly that the knowledge derived from revelation and from reason is essentially the same, admits that reason is capable of reaching the divinely revealed truth by its own powers, and indeed he sees the acquisition of truth by rational means as a religious obligation. And Saadya argues that where the literal meaning of a biblical text is in conflict with reason, it is scripture which has to be reinterpreted: thus (albeit in a limited sense) reason may have stronger claims on us than tradition. Precisely because man is capable of reasoning, he is obliged to utilize this faculty to the full in pursuit of knowledge. This principle was accepted and developed further by subsequent Jewish thinkers, as it was also by Muslim and eventually by Christian religious philosophers. In fact the majority of Jewish thinkers concentrated their efforts on the philosophical justification of Judaism, and were content to leave the investigation of wider questions in physics and metaphysics to their Muslim counterparts.

Even among the Jews, however, there were those who felt drawn to the philosophical exploration of all the mysteries of the universe. This urge is felt most vividly in the work of Solomon Ibn Gabirol, who besides being a philosopher was also a powerful and gifted poet. His major philosophical work, *The Fountain of Life*, which later came to exercise an important influence on Christian scholastic thought, is a work of pure metaphysics, divorced from any particular religious context. The same metaphysical ideas are expressed in religious terms in his long liturgical poem *The Royal Crown*, which in some rites has been incorporated in the prayers for the Day of Atonement. To the apparently intractable question how the imperfect world which we know can derive from God, who is a perfect, utterly spiritual being, Ibn Gabirol responds with a typically Neoplatonic theory of emanations: from the Divine Will (which is in a sense identical with God, yet distinct in its outward effects) there emanate the two basic principles of 'general matter' and 'general form', giving rise to a whole chain of emanations which ends with the present world, in which the Divine Will is still present. Man is a microcosm, partaking of both the intelligible and the corporeal worlds, and so able to grasp the spiritual, immaterial forms by his own powers. The details of this sophisticated system are far from clear, but the intention is obvious: to preserve the link between God and man while safeguarding the absolute perfection of God. The same intention was to give rise to the emanationist system of the Kabbalah, and Neoplatonic emanationism also pervaded the rival philosophical system, Aristotelianism, which dominated Jewish religious philosophy from about the middle of the twelfth century, in large measure thanks to the towering figure of Moses Maimonides.

That Maimonides represents a peak in the history of Jewish theology is not in doubt. He gave Jewish rationalism its classical formulation, casting all his predecessors in the shade and pointing the way for all his successors, even for those who disagreed with his views. His achievement is less that of an original genius attempting a new departure than that of a brilliant, creative synthesizer. The dominant philosophy of his day, as developed by a succession of highly gifted Muslim thinkers, was a form of Aristotelianism deeply marked by Neoplatonist ideas. Its strength was its belief in the power of human reason to achieve knowledge and to organize this knowledge systematically. The religious tradition, on the other hand, was rooted in divine revelation embodied in the Bible. Maimonides gave full weight and validity to both revelation and reason, without trying to subordinate one to the other. Nor did he try to argue that religion and philosophy were simply two different and equally valid ways of looking at the same thing, or that they were two separate domains, with different concerns and not really at odds with each other. He had a strong belief in the power of prophecy and revelation, and especially the revelation granted to Moses, the greatest of the prophets; but he had an equally strong belief in the power of reason, and in the exercise of reason as the supreme human task. In a vivid parable, he likened God to a king in his palace, whose subjects are wandering around in search of him. The majority of Jews, who simply carry out the commandments of the Torah, have not even set eyes on the palace. The students of the Talmud, who have no philosophical training and do not attempt to prove their faith by reason, have reached the palace but merely walk round the outside of it. Those who have embarked on a philosophical training have already entered the antechamber of the palace; when their studies are complete and they have learnt the limit of what can be known and proved, then they are inside the palace with the king. This devaluation of Talmudic study, commonly regarded as the crown of Jewish education, naturally provoked a bitterly hostile reaction in some circles. But Maimonides also insisted that there were strict limits on the extent that reason could serve as a guide. Beyond those limits, the only true guide is revelation, mediated by tradition. The most celebrated example of his limitation of the role of philosophical teaching is his endorsement of the biblical idea of the creation of the world, in the face of the Aristotelian doctrine of the eternity of the world, which he showed to be insufficiently established by rational proof.

This radical departure from Aristotelian doctrine opened the door to a real synthesis between biblical religion and Aristotelian philosophy. It was this achievement which won him his fame among subsequent thinkers, Jewish, Muslim and Christian, as the man who established Jewish faith on a sound philosophical basis. His carefully reasoned expositions also gave a boost to philosophical thought among a wider educated Jewish public. His main philosophical work, the *Guide for the Perplexed*, came to be regarded as the philosophical exposition of Judaism *par excellence*, and his brief formulation of the Thirteen Principles of the Jewish faith came to be regarded as a kind of creed, even being incorporated in simplified form, as we have seen, in the synagogue liturgy. But the very success of the Maimonidean synthesis unleashed a violent reaction which shook Jewish intellectual life to its roots. Among philosophers there were different schools of thought, and considerable disagreements over both general principles and specific points of detail. Great as was the authority of Maimonides, several of his followers took him severely to task: thus Gersonides (1288–1344), one of the outstanding Jewish intellects of the Middle Ages, felt that he had compromised Aristotelian principles too far in the direction of Neoplatonism, while Hasdai Crescas (*c.* 1340–1410) put forward a penetrating philosophical critique of Aristotelianism itself. These differences among philosophers did not challenge the basic principle of free philosophical enquiry. In some circles, however, the whole basis of religious rationalism was attacked. In some cases this was a reaction against excessive rationalism and its strong appeal; others critics, such as the rabbis of northern France, who were solid in their condemnation of Maimonides, lived in a different cultural milieu, where Talmudic studies reigned supreme and the study of philosophy had never gained a foothold. Whatever the motives for the attacks, they were pursued with vigour and acrimony, and so heated did the controversy become that in 1232 the *Guide for the Perplexed* was publicly burned in Montpellier by Christians, allegedly at the instigation of the anti-Maimonidean party. The anti-rationalist ferment unleashed by the Maimonidean controversy had an enduring effect on Jewish attitudes, and philosophical enquiry was effectively suppressed through much of the Jewish world for centuries.

It was precisely at this time that the theosophical system of the Kabbalah emerged in Provence and northern Spain, the areas where the controversy was waged most fiercely. We have already seen that Kabbalah is not to be viewed simply as a reaction against philosophical rationalism. Its characteristic beliefs betray the influence of Neoplatonist philosophy, and underlying all the elaborations is a desire for an understanding of the nature of God which is not far removed in its basic essentials from that of the philosophers. In any account of the medieval Jewish tradition of speculation about the nature of God and his relationship with the world the kabbalistic contribution cannot be ignored.

In what sense can this tradition be considered an authentic Jewish tradition, and what is its place within the wider context of Judaism? In the first place, it must be said that both philosophical investigation and Kabbalah answered to a real need on the part of some Jews to achieve a better understanding of theological questions. In the case of philosophy, it was a need which was shared with non-Jews, that is with Muslims and Christians, and the outcome was not so much an internal Jewish tradition, even one fed by currents of thought coming from outside, as the participation by Jews in a wider debate involving intellectuals of all three faiths. The Jewish participants, while drawing on the work of their Jewish predecessors, essentially responded to stimuli and challenges raised by their contemporaries and contributed in their turn to the discussion which transcended confessional frontiers. The case of Kabbalah was different: although it is certainly nourished by external influences, it is a uniquely Jewish synthesis, and moreover it is a genuine tradition, in the sense that it was transmitted directly from teacher to pupil, each generation extending and developing what it inherited from the previous one. Both tendencies attracted a large following, and this is particularly true of Kabbalah, which was spread over a remarkably wide geographical area, from Spain to the Middle

East and eventually to northern Europe, and also succeeded in becoming, in certain of its forms, a truly popular movement. On the other hand it has to be admitted that the appeal of both tendencies was strictly limited, in a variety of ways.

In the first place, both have a deliberately esoteric focus. In their different ways, they offer their treasures to initiates, to people who are prepared to make a commitment beyond the ordinary demands of the Jewish religion. In the case of Kabbalah, this is an emotional or spiritual commitment. The Kabbalists commonly imposed limitations on the people to whom their teachings could be communicated, specifying for example a minimum age or a certain level of ethical qualities. In the case of philosophy, too, a minimum age was sometimes stipulated, but the essential commitment was an intellectual one. Whereas the Kabbalists tended to see their teachings as a secret revelation which was not to be made public, the philosophers tended to see theirs as being beyond the reach of ordinary people. Even Maimonides, who as we have seen asserts that an apprehension of philosophical truth is necessary for anyone who would approach close to God, couches his teachings in the *Guide for the Perplexed* in such obscure terms that they are only accessible to a narrow circle of initiates, even if he offers his Thirteen Principles as a bare summary for those who have to rely on faith rather than intellectual power.

Inevitably, therefore, the insights of philosophy and Kabbalah were only directly available to a minority of Jews, an intellectual and to some degree social élite. However much their exponents regarded them as a superior alternative to the established religious forms and the conventional approaches to God, they were unable or unwilling to make them into *the* authoritative and authentic way for all Jews, as the Talmudic rabbis (no less élitist in their outlook) had succeeded in doing for the Halakhah. It must be added that geographically the influence of philosophy was very limited. It was effectively confined to the Muslim world and adjacent parts of Christian Europe (Spain and Provence and to a lesser extent Italy), and even within this area it only flourished in a few centres. It never succeeded in penetrating the important Jewish intellectual centres of northern France and Germany, and its influence in Byzantium seems to have been slight.

An important factor not unrelated to the foregoing is the strong opposition which both tendencies aroused. We have already noticed the strong hostility to rationalism which was a feature of the Maimonidean controversy. It was this anti-rational attitude which became dominant and, as it were, normative in Judaism, and it is still felt in some circles to the present day. Kabbalah, too, was the object of considerable opposition, as the writings of the Kabbalists themselves testify, and even though they were far more successful than the philosophers in over-coming the opposition (being able to link their beliefs to popular religious sentiment) it persisted and was always liable to flare up, particularly at moments of political and social crisis.

The upshot of all this is that what we have broadly and rather loosely termed the theological tradition in Judaism never man-aged to establish itself in a central position. Medieval Judaism continued to be dominated by Talmudic study focused on Halakhah, and all rival schools of thought had to accept a secondary role, being viewed with suspicion if not outright con-demnation. It is significant that Maimonides was remembered primarily as a halakhic authority; indeed it is likely that had it not been for the respect in which he was held as a halakhist he would have been definitively condemned, and his philosophical work consigned to oblivion. This was the fate which befell Ibn Gabirol: his enduring fame in Jewish circles rested on his poems, many of which were incorporated in the synagogue liturgy. His *Fountain of Life*, in Latin translation, was popular among the Christian scholastics, who imagined that its author (known to them under the garbled name Avicebron) was a Muslim. It was only in 1845 that the French Jewish scholar Solomon Munk discovered that Avicebron and Ibn Gabirol were one and the same person.

The actual influence of philosophy and Kabbalah on Judaism has been variously assessed. Neither approach, it is true, succeeded in establishing an 'official' Jewish theology, and if that was their aim (which is debatable) they must be deemed to have failed. They did, however, serve a valuable purpose in pointing the way for many Jews to an orderly intellectual apprehension of theological questions which Talmudic Judaism was unable to supply. Moreover, the Kabbalists reached considerable agree-ment on the description of God's nature and activity, and even if their description was not accepted in wider Jewish circles as in any sense an 'orthodox' Jewish theology, yet for a very long time (at least from about 1500 to 1800) it had no real rival. As for the philosophers, they made their own important contribution to the kabbalistic conception of God (most notably through the Neoplatonic theory of emanations, which is fundamental to the kabbalistic system), and they also laid the groundwork for later rational investigation of Jewish beliefs. Halakhah, which remained the most characteristic and broadly accepted expression of Judaism throughout the Middle Ages, was essentially concerned with practical questions and therefore largely immune to the direct interference of theological speculation, although there is interesting evidence of kabbalistic influence both on the official formulation of Halakhah and, to a much larger extent, on popular practices. But perhaps the most important influence of both philosophy and Kabbalah on official Judaism is to be felt in the liturgy. Although the main prayers were jealously guarded against revision, and so continued to present an essentially rabbinic view of God, there was ample scope for the importation of current ideas in the hymns and liturgical poems which came to occupy an increasing part in the worship of the synagogue. There are many examples of the intrusion of philosophical ideas into the hymnology of the synagogue, and likewise a very large number of kabbalistic hymns, several of which have survived the radical pruning of the liturgy in a more radical age and retained their popularity to this day. Through the synagogue worship these esoteric beliefs filtered through to a wider Jewish public, and so played a permanent part in moulding popular Jewish belief side by side with the older rabbinic ideas.

Philosophical speculation never entirely died out in Judaism, but from the fourteenth century on it moved in ever decreasing circles until it re-emerged in the eighteenth century in the context of the European Enlightenment. The only noteworthy feature of the intervening period is the influence of the medieval philosophers, such as Maimonides, Gersonides and Crescas, on the thought of Spinoza. But Spinoza's philosophy, even if it has some of its roots in earlier Jewish philosophy, marks such a radical break with Judaism that it can hardly be represented either as a development of the earlier tradition or as a genuinely Jewish search for understanding of God. In fact Spinoza conducts a thoroughgoing attack on the very foundations of religion, and rejects any attempt to derive the material world from a transcendent God. Although Spinoza retains the word 'God', and indeed gives it a central part in the exposition of his ideas, his God is far removed from the God of traditional Judaism, who is a personal agent distinct from the world which he creates. Spinoza's God is an impersonal and infinite substance, and everything is 'in' God, deriving its being from his existence and subject to strict laws of necessity. Whether his system is better described as 'pantheism' or as 'atheism' is hardly an important question. What does matter is that, although superficially it may appear to preserve the classical beliefs in a single, unique God on whom everything depends, in reality it is totally at odds with all theistic belief. His works are not addressed specifically to Jews, but to European thinkers at large, and they take their place within the wider history of modern philosophy. It was only after Jewish thinkers had begun to participate in that wider history that the influence of Spinoza began to be felt in Jewish thought.

It is significant, for example, that Moses Mendelssohn expressed a deep interest in, and sympathy for, the ideas of Spinoza, most notably in his last work, *Morgenstunden* (*Morning Hours*), in which he demonstrated the rationality of the belief in the existence of God. This work is not directed particularly to Jews, but to an enlightened German readership, and Mendelssohn embraces wholeheartedly the rationalism of the Enlightenment, with its belief in a universal moral law grounded in rational religious truth. Mendelssohn agreed with Spinoza in allocating rational truth and religion to separate spheres, but unlike Spinoza he upheld the value of religion, and remained a faithful and observant Jew to the end of his life. Like the medieval Jewish philosophers from Saadya on, whose arguments he uses, Mendelssohn believes firmly in the revelation at Sinai, the validity of which was guaranteed, as it was for Saadya, by the fact that it was witnessed by a whole people. Like the earlier Jewish philosophers, and like the Christian philosophers of his day, he maintains the congruence of revelation and reason. However, he does not agree that revelation transmits and validates doctrines which are independently accessible through reasoning. He distinguishes between the universal truths which are accessible through reason, and therefore available to all men, and the commandments of the Torah, revealed at Sinai to the Jewish people and binding on them alone. The divinely revealed law is supplementary to the universal religion of reason with which the religious beliefs of Judaism as a whole are in agreement.

Mendelssohn's Jewish successors continued to grapple, as he had, with the relationship of revelation to the religion of reason, although his categorization of Judaism as 'revealed legislation' found little favour. Essentially they were continuing the quest pursued by the medieval philosophers, but in the context of Kantian and post-Kantian German philosophy. Whereas the medieval philosophers had been concerned to harmonize revelation and reason which were both understood as supremely and equally authoritative, the post-Enlightenment thinkers permitted themselves to question the divine authority of revelation. Nevertheless, they resisted the full force of German idealism in their understanding of the concept of God, and remained remarkably faithful to the traditional Jewish beliefs in a free, transcendent creator God who allows man moral freedom. They tended to focus their investigations in the sphere of ethics rather than metaphysics. The effort to identify Judaism with the religion of reason found its last and fullest expression in the work of Hermann Cohen, and especially in his last book, *The Religion of Reason Drawn from the Sources of Judaism*, published posthumously in 1919. Here Cohen moves beyond the ethical idealism of his earlier work, in which God is conceived as an impersonal idea, towards a thoroughgoing account of Judaism in which God once again becomes a personal being, existing apart from man and involved in a relationship with him, which can be expressed as a relationship of love. Even in this last work, however, which is imbued with a rich understanding of Judaism and a profound sympathy with religious feeling, God remains an idea rather than an independent reality: there is an irreducible tension between the God of philosophy and the God of religion.

Hermann Cohen marks an end, but he also points the way towards a new beginning. The ideas he began to develop in his last work inspired a younger generation to seek beyond the well-worn paths of philosophic rationalism to a more emotionally satisfying perception of the nature of God and his relationship with man. The greatest of Cohen's disciples was Franz Rosenzweig (1886–1929), whose book *The Star of Redemption*, begun on army postcards sent home to his mother from military service in the

First World War, has come to be recognized as the most influential work of Jewish theology of modern times. Rosenzweig begins from real human experience, and more precisely from the fear of death. Since philosophy cannot cure man of this fear, philosophy is false, and so is its pretension to reduce everything to a single principle. A new way of thinking is needed, which will give full weight to man's own needs, and to the natural perception of God, man and the world as three separate entities. He examines each in turn, proceeding by way of negation to assertion, and then considers the relationship of each element with the others. The triad God–man–world leads in this way to the triad creation (seen in the relation of God to the world)–revelation (seen in the relation of God to man)–redemption (seen in the relation of man to the world). Rosenzweig symbolizes the conjunction of these two triads in the six-pointed star, a symbol of Judaism and the source of the book's title. Within this simple structure there is contained a vast wealth of suggestive insights, developed through personal experience rather than traditional doctrines or logical arguments, and couched in a deliberately oblique and poetic language. Language as a means of communication plays a cardinal role in Rosenzweig's thought, as does love, which is fundamental to the relationship between God and man. *The Star of Redemption* is not a description or analysis of Judaism—it is much more wide-ranging than that, and much more personal—but it contains within itself a novel and creative reappraisal of the spirit of Judaism as exemplified in its beliefs and practices. Rosenzweig opens the door to a new, existentialist philosophy of religion; in fact he clearly anticipated many of the principles and ideas of existentialism. Unfortunately his book did not have the immediate influence it deserved: the existentialists ignored it, thinking of it as a purely Jewish work, while the German Jewish intellectuals who might have developed his ideas further perished or were dispersed in the Nazi nightmare. But through the writings of survivors who were associated with him (such as S. H. Bergman, Nahum Glatzer, A. J. Heschel, Ignaz Maybaum and Ernst Simon) his thought has gradually percolated through to a wider Jewish public, and the brilliant English translation of the *Star* by William W. Hallo (published in 1970) has made his words available to a younger generation no longer familiar with German.

Martin Buber was a friend and close associate of Rosenzweig, and his well-known philosophy of dialogue, like Rosenzweig's 'new thinking', is based on personal experience and relationship. Buber's God, characterized as the 'Eternal You', is known not through doctrinal formulation or metaphysical speculation but through personal encounter. It is the encounter with the Eternal You that constitutes revelation, and this revelation, which has no objective content, is open to anyone who is prepared to relate fully to the world around him. Buber's ideas represent an extreme reaction against the traditional quest for a rational understanding of God, and give voice to a newer search for a more personally fulfilling explanation. Although in a formal sense it is no doubt true to say that they have so far had a more marked impact on Christian than on Jewish thinkers, they have also answered to the unformulated need of many Jews either disillusioned with institutional religion or bewildered and repelled by the traditional teachings about God.

The classical Jewish teachings about God have had to face one of their most momentous challenges ever in the events of the Nazi holocaust. How can the belief in a perfectly free, perfectly good, perfectly just God, active in history, caring for his creation, and with a special interest in the people of Israel, have willed or even tolerated deliberate evil on such a scale, and involving the torture and brutal killing of a large part of the Jewish people, including many rabbis, pious people and even newborn babies? Questions like these cannot easily be answered or silenced by the detached observations of philosophers about man's free will or by pietistic homilies about the purifying effects of suffering and atonement. Jewish history contains many records of persecutions and massacres, but there are certain events which in their enormity transcend the usual categories. The destruction of the first Temple was such an event; so was the destruction of the second Temple, and in later times perhaps the expulsion from Spain and the Cossack massacres in Poland. All these events have left lasting scars in the collective Jewish psyche, and they all gave a violent jolt to Jewish theological beliefs. Some of the survivors of the Nazi destruction have attempted to assimilate this latest event into the chain of earlier disasters; but for others it is too enormous and overwhelming an experience to be fitted into a pattern, and has to be encountered as a unique challenge to traditional faith.

The most radical response is the denial of the traditional belief in a personal, loving God. This approach is associated particularly with the name of Richard Rubenstein, who expounded his 'death of God' theology in his book *After Auschwitz*, published in 1966. It has to be added, however, that for Rubenstein the recognition of God's absence from Auschwitz is only a beginning. Having rejected his illusions about God, man is called to face up to his existential situation, and find his own meaning in the meaninglessness of existence. The Jews can find a special meaning in the existence of the Jewish people and the forms of the Jewish religion. Rubenstein's approach therefore has something in common with the naturalistic theology pioneered by Mordecai Kaplan, whose view of Jewish existence having a validity independent of God was set out as long ago as 1934 in his book *Judaism as a Civilization*.

Rubenstein certainly articulates the instinctive reaction of many people who experienced the holocaust, either as victims or as onlookers; his theological elaboration of this reaction, however, has remained virtually unique: most Jewish theological writers have resisted drawing such a drastic and revolutionary lesson from the awful event. Some prefer to see it as a mystery that cannot be comprehended. Emil Fackenheim, for example, has refused to allow any theological explanation of the holocaust: there is no possible theory of God's goodness or of his activity in history which can make sense of it. Building on Buber's philosophy of encounter, Fackenheim goes on to draw a positive message from the catastrophe: it is a moment of revelation for the Jewish people. A commanding voice sounds forth from the gas chambers of Auschwitz, and the command is 'You shall survive'—so as not to offer Hitler a posthumous victory. The Orthodox theologian Eliezer Berkovits, who is severely critical of Buber's philosophy, also underlines the theological mystery of Auschwitz, but he expresses it in terms of the age-old Jewish idea that God sometimes inexplicably 'hides his face'. Seeking for an explanation of what happened within the framework of traditional Jewish teaching about God, Berkovits stresses the belief in man's freedom: since God patiently tolerates evil, there must be some who suffer at the hands of wicked men. Auschwitz points not to the 'death of God', but to his forbearance and mercy. For Berkovits, in fact, the holocaust is not a unique event, but an outstanding example of a universal theological problem, the problem of suffering. And he sees in the continued existence of the Jewish people, despite their long record of suffering, a convincing testimony to the presence of God in history despite his hiddenness.

Ignaz Maybaum, a disciple of Rosenzweig, also looks for the meaning of the holocaust within the history of the Jewish people (and indeed within the wider history of European civilization), and like Berkovits he refuses to see it as a unique and unprecedented happening. Like the destruction of the two Temples, it is an epoch-making event, which sweeps away the past and opens the way for human progress. Thus Maybaum, too, discovers a hopeful message in the nightmare.

These contemporary theologians, wrestling in their different ways with the problems posed for Jewish belief by the unbelievable horror of Auschwitz, appear to be not so much attempting to reconcile faith with reason in the manner of the medieval philosophers as to preserve the essence of the biblical and rabbinic image of God in the context of an exploration of existential responses to Jewish history. Their work testifies to the inherent flexibility of Jewish theology, and to its somewhat nebulous quality, which derives from its lack of centrality within Judaism as a whole. It is often observed that in Judaism God, Torah and Israel form a tightly-interwoven complex, and just as none of the three elements can be removed without damaging the whole, none of them can be exalted too high above the others. God is essential to Judaism, and to talk about God we need to have some concept of him. But the idea of God cannot be pursued in a vacuum. The experience of the Nazi holocaust, followed by the reestablishment of a Jewish state in Israel, has brought Jewish theologians back from a mood of universal humanism to focus on the reality of the existence of the Jewish people, and from a concern with metaphysics to an interest in history as the arena of God's activity.

9

The Eschatological Tradition

You are eternally powerful, Lord, you are the Reviver of the Dead and a great rescuer, loving sustainer of the living and merciful reviver of the dead, supporter of the falling, healer of the sick, liberator of captives, and trustworthy to those who sleep in the earth. Whose power can compare with yours, and who is like you a king dealing out death and life and rescue? And you are trusted to revive the dead. Blessed are you, Lord, Reviver of the Dead . . .

Sound the great trumpet for our liberation, raise high the banner to summon home our exiles, and gather us together from the four corners of the world. Blessed are you, Lord, Gatherer of his scattered people Israel.

Restore our judges as in former times and our counsellors as in the beginning, remove from us sorrow and sighing, and rule over us yourself alone, Lord, with love and compassion, judging us justly. Blessed are you, Lord, Lover of justice and judgment . . .

And return with compassion to your city Jerusalem, and dwell within it as you have promised; rebuild it forever, quickly in our own lifetime, and set up there again the throne of David soon. Blessed are you, Lord, Builder of Jerusalem.

Make the offshoot of your servant David spring up soon, and guide him to victory by your rescuing help, for we wait for your rescue all day long. Blessed are you, Lord, Victorious Rescuer.

From the daily *Amidah*

Most religions draw a contrast between an ideal human existence and life as we know and live it, and Judaism is no exception. Many religions, and here again Judaism is no exception, associate this ideal existence with the destiny which is supposed to await each individual human being after death, and which will bring, at least for the fortunate few, release from the imperfections and limitations of life in this world. But Judaism also acknowledges a strong sense of dissatisfaction with life on a larger scale, with the life of the whole people of Israel or indeed the whole of human-kind, and looks forward to a time when this, too, will be per-fected. This hope is a fundamental and characteristic feature of Judaism. It is already present in the Bible, which begins with Paradise Lost and looks forward, as it were, to Paradise Regained at the end of time, and it has been a constant comfort and encouragement to Jews through seemingly endless trials and setbacks.

This hopeful attitude must certainly not be understood as in any sense undervaluing life as we know it. This life, with all its frustrations and tribulations, is regarded as a precious gift from God, and we have seen that even the urge to evil can be assessed in a positive sense. There are many fine sermons, too, on the theme of suffering, which stress the strength and nobility that it can bring: suffering can even be described as an 'affliction of love', as testifying, in some sense, to the love relationship between God and man. But alongside this positive evaluation of life there is a keen sense of the shortcomings of this life, with its frustrations and disappointments, its injustice and exploitation of man by man, when measured against the perfection which is perceived in God and which man, too, is deemed capable of achieving.

It must not be imagined, however, that Judaism offers any clear teaching about the destiny which lies in wait either for the individual or for the people of Israel or the human race in the inscrutable future. For the future *is* inscrutable, and the accepted sources of knowledge, whether experience, or reason, or revela-tion, offer no clear guidance about what is to come. The only certainty is that each man must die—beyond that we can only guess.

The ancient rabbis inherited from the Bible a variety of ideas about the future, and to these they added beliefs derived from other sources. From the Bible they inherited first and foremost the idea of the Covenant, that ancient and inviolable bond between God and the people of Israel which guaranteed victory and prosperity if the people obeyed God's commandments and utter desolation if they abandoned them. But even in the midst of captivity and degradation God would always remember his people, and if they turned to him he would restore their fortunes.

'Even if you are scattered to the furthest part of heaven, from there the Lord your God will gather you in and bring you back. He will take you back to the land which your forefathers possessed, and you will possess it; he will make you prosper, and make you more numerous than your forefathers were.' Clearly linked to this belief is the prophetic message of the Day of the Lord, a direct divine intervention to bring to an end oppression and exploitation, religious indifference and arrogance, and to reward the righteous and institute a reign of peace and justice. There are other visions, too, in the biblical prophets: the restoration of the kingdom of David, and the establishment of Jerusalem as a centre to which all the nations will throng in search of the God of Israel and his teachings. There is not one consistent belief here, but many mingled themes. Will the Day of the Lord be a time of exaltation for Israel and punishment for its enemies, or will Israel too be judged? Will there be a strong leader or redeemer to execute God's will, or will God act directly? Will this intervention be, as it were, a natural or a supernatural event, and is the reign of peace and justice to be conceived in natural or supernatural terms? Will Israel have dominion over the other nations, or will national differences be overcome and all share alike in the blessings of the new age? When will the new age come, and how will it be recognized? To these and other similar questions there was no clear answer.

To the various biblical teachings the rabbis added others which were derived from different sources, and they also introduced refinements and developments of their own. One important area of development concerned survival after death. The Bible had very little to say on this subject, but by the time of the rabbis two distinct ideas had made strong inroads among Jews. One idea, which is probably derived from Greek thought, is that of the immortal soul, trapped, as it were, in a perishable body. The death of the body liberates the soul, which returns to its creator. The second idea, which is thought to be of Persian origin, is that of resurrection: death is only an apparent ending, and at some future time the dead will be brought back to life. This idea can be traced back to the period of martyrdom at the time of the Maccabean Revolt in the second century BCE. It had taken very strong root by rabbinic times, although we know that some Jews vehemently opposed it. The rabbis reserve their extreme condemnation for anyone who denies the resurrection, and they go to great lengths to prove that it is actually mentioned in the Bible. Faith in the resurrection is expressed uncompromisingly in the prayer quoted at the head of this chapter, in which God is called 'Reviver of the Dead'. It has been plausibly suggested that this prayer was introduced into the service as a test, to prevent those who denied the resurrection from leading the worship. Originally, the two ideas of immortality and resurrection are quite different and even contradictory, but in rabbinic thought they are combined: the soul departs from the body at death, but is returned to it at the resurrection. This thought is expressed succinctly in an ancient prayer which is recited in the morning service: 'My God, the soul which you have placed within me is pure. You created and formed it and breathed it into me, you preserve it within me, and you will take it away from me but will replace it in me at a future time . . .' This idea is linked to another rabbinic teaching which is not found in the Bible, and that is the teaching that men's good and bad actions are rewarded and punished not in this life but after death, whether immediately or at the subsequent resurrection.

There are three other ideas which are very prominent in all rabbinic teaching about the future: the Messiah, the Kingdom of God, and the Coming Age. The term Messiah, meaning 'the anointed one', is applied in the Bible to a king or high priest who is anointed with oil as a sign of his induction to office. It is not used for the future redeemer, although the idea of a descendant of King David who will usher in the period of national redemption is certainly found in some of the prophetic writings. The rabbis regularly use the term Messiah to speak of the redeemer, and they also refer to the age of redemption as 'the days of the Messiah'. At first they looked forward eagerly to his coming, and some of them involved themselves in popular Messianic movements aimed at shrugging off the yoke of Rome. In later times they tended to discourage attempts to hasten the coming of the Messiah or to calculate the appointed time, but the hope of Messianic redemption did not dim.

The term 'Kingdom of God' is also found commonly in the rabbinic writings, and it is used in a number of ways which cannot easily be differentiated. Frequently it is contrasted with the earthly kingdom, which for the early rabbis meant the Roman empire. Although it can suggest simply a personal submission to the rule of God, the contrast with Roman rule readily implies the age of redemption. This is the sense in which it is used in the Aramaic prayer known as the *Kaddish*, which occupies a prominent place in the synagogue service and is also recited by mourners: 'Magnified and sanctified be his great name in the world which he created according to his will. May he establish his kingdom in your life and days, and in the lifetime of all the house of Israel, speedily and soon, and say Amen . . .'

The idea is represented more elaborately in a prayer which in the Ashkenazi rite concludes every service:

So we hope for you, Lord our God, that we may soon behold your splendid might, to remove idols from the world so that all false gods are eradicated, to perfect the world by the Kingdom of the Almighty so that all mankind will call on your name, and to turn all evildoers in the world towards yourself. All dwellers on earth will recognize and know that it is to you that every knee must bend and every tongue swear. Before you, Lord our God, they will bend and prostrate themselves, and to your glorious name ascribe honour; they will all accept the yoke of your Kingdom, and you will reign over them soon for ever and ever. For kingship is yours, and for all ages you reign in glory, as it is written in your Torah: 'The Lord reigns for ever and ever.' And it is said: 'The Lord shall be king over all the world; in that day the Lord shall be one, and his name one.'

Implied here is the belief that earthly rulers are usurping a power which properly belongs to God alone, and that this denial of God's rule leads directly to the worship of false gods and material idols. The recognition of God's kingdom will thus bring all mankind to the worship of the One God.

The Coming Age (*Olam ha-Ba*, sometimes translated 'World to Come') is distinguished from the days of the Messiah: the days of the Messiah are imagined as essentially this-worldly, whereas the Coming Age involves a fundamental change in the order of creation. As one rabbi put it, 'The days of the Messiah do not differ at all from the present except that Israel will no longer be in bondage to the kingdoms of the world.' But if some information can be gleaned, however dimly, about the days of the Messiah from the visions of the prophets, when it comes to the Coming Age we are completely in the dark. To quote another rabbi, 'Every prophet prophesied only for the days of the Messiah; but as for the Coming Age, no eye has seen what God has prepared for those who wait for him.' This does not prevent the rabbis, however, from placing a strong emphasis on the Coming Age in their teaching, and even from speculating about its character. 'In the Coming Age there is no eating or drinking, no reproduction or business, no jealousy or hatred or competition, but the virtuous sit with crowns on their heads feasting on the brightness of the Shekhinah.' In other words, all those features of human life which derive from man's animal nature and the influence of the inclination to evil will be removed, and men will be like angels, living eternally in a kind of sublime impassivity. It is characteristic of Judaism that this hoped-for culmination of human existence, the ultimate reward of virtue with its intimate communion with God, is often contrasted with the present age in a way which almost implies that this life is to be preferred: at least it offers certain experiences which we will be denied in the Coming Age. So one teacher declares, 'Better is one hour of repentance and good deeds in this age than all the life of the Coming Age', while another states that a man will have to give an account on Judgment Day of every good thing which he might have enjoyed and did not. It is thus no exaggeration to say that, despite the profound yearning for the hereafter, Judaism is a thoroughly this-worldly religion.

If it is possible to condense the rabbinic views about the hereafter into a brief summary (and it might be objected with justice that any such attempt is foredoomed to failure as a gross oversimplification), it might go something like this: After death the souls of the virtuous are dispatched to the Garden of Eden, while those of the wicked undergo a period of punishment in Gehinnom. The coming of the Messiah will be preceded by various social and economic crises; then the prophet Elijah will return, a great trumpet will sound and the exiles will be gathered in; there will follow a cataclysmic war, known as the war of Gog and Magog, and after that the world will be renewed in the Messianic era, which will be an era of peace and harmony on earth. Eventually the dead will be resurrected and judged together with the living, and those who survive the judgment will live eternally in the Coming Age.

In the Middle Ages, under deteriorating external conditions, the yearning for Messianic redemption became progressively stronger. The prayers and hymns of this period communicate a sense of real urgency, and on numerous occasions the longing for redemption broke out into direct action, when Messianic figures gathered bands of enthusiastic followers around them. The most celebrated of these figures is Shabbetai Zvi, who proclaimed himself publicly as the Messiah in the synagogue of Smyrna in December 1665, and whose fame spread rapidly throughout the Jewish world. Great was the disappointment when two years later he adopted Islam to save his life, but some of his most fervent followers continued to believe in him even after his death. Shabbetai Zvi is only one name on the long rollcall of Messianic claimants, which extends back to Roman times and includes such colourful figures as Abu Issa of Isfahan, who led 10,000 followers into battle against Abbasid forces in the eighth century, David Alroy of Kurdistan who in the twelfth century staged a revolt against the Seljuk sultan, Solomon Molkho, who was burnt at the stake in Mantua in 1532, and Jacob Frank, who was baptized amid royal pomp in the cathedral of Warsaw in 1759. In each case revolutionary fervour and eschatological hope gave way to baffled disillusionment. And in each case the Messianic claims were received with suspicion or downright rejection by the established Jewish religious leadership, mindful both of their delicate political responsibilities and of the rabbinic warnings against calculating or hastening the end.

We have interesting information from Maimonides about the different views which were held by Jews in the twelfth century on the subject of rewards and punishments in the hereafter. Complaining that observant Jews hold widely differing and totally confused ideas on the subject, Maimonides distinguishes five different groups. The first group maintain that the good are rewarded in the Garden of Eden and the bad are punished in Gehinnom. The Garden of Eden is 'a place where people eat and drink without effort, where houses are built of precious stones and beds are spread with silk, where rivers flow with wine and aromatic oils, and so forth', while Gehinnom is 'a place of blazing fire, where bodies are burned and people suffer various pains and torments which would take too long to describe'. The second group believe that the reward of the virtuous is to live to see the days of the Messiah, when 'ready-made clothes and ready-baked bread will spring from the earth, and suchlike impossibilities'.

The third group believe that the virtuous man will be rewarded by being brought back to life after his death, 'to rejoin his family, eat and drink, and never die again'. The fourth group maintain that the reward for virtue is 'physical peace and fulfilment of worldly desires in this world, such as good harvests, wealth, large families, physical health, peace, confidence, a sovereign Jewish king and dominion over our enemies'. The fifth group combine all these various beliefs, and look forward to the coming of the Messiah and the resurrection of the dead who will enter the Garden of Eden and live for ever. Maimonides quite obviously has a low regard for all these opinions, which he ascribes in the main to an over-literal interpretation of the words of the Bible and the rabbis. He also complains that hardly anyone takes the idea of the Coming Age seriously, or asks what it refers to.

Maimonides himself insists that the biblical and rabbinic teachings have to be understood figuratively, and that the ultimate reward, which he identifies with the Coming Age, is the purely spiritual reunion of the immortal soul with God, while the ultimate punishment for evildoing is the annihilation of the soul. The resurrection of the dead Maimonides describes as a fundamental and essential principle of Judaism, but it will only apply to the righteous. The way to achieve the eternal life of the Coming Age is to observe all the commandments of the Torah out of perfect love and for no ulterior purpose. The days of the Messiah are entirely this-worldly. The Messiah, a descendant of King Solomon, will be a great and powerful king who will gather in the exiles and restore Jewish sovereignty over the Land of Israel. He will eventually die, and his descendants will rule after him; their rule will last for thousands of years, since a perfect society does not easily disintegrate. Ordinary life will not change, except that everything will become easier and people will live longer because they will have no worries. The people of Israel, being relieved of the obstacle of subjection to the world empires, will be free to perform all the laws of the Torah, and thus improve their chances of achieving the spiritual bliss of the Coming Age.

It has to be said that Maimonides' views were not universally accepted (as he himself concedes), and he was severely criticized on a number of counts, for example for his naturalistic view of the Messianic era and for undervaluing the concepts of the resurrection of the dead and the immortality of the soul. The idea of the transmigration of souls (*gilgul*) came to be widely believed in some circles, and the Kabbalists, in particular, developed complex views on the different kinds of soul and their fate after the death of the body. The Lurianic Kabbalah, with its doctrine of the 'breaking of the vessels', introduced a new dimension into Jewish Messianism. It is man's task to complete the rectification or perfection (*tikkun*) of the cosmos by performing *mitzvot* with the correct mystical intention, so as to release the trapped sparks and restore them to their divine source. When this process is complete, redemption will come not only to mankind but also to the whole cosmos and, in a sense, to God himself.

The early Hasidim developed this doctrine even further, teaching that each individual has his own allotted task of *tikkun*, his own sparks which he must liberate. If he fails to complete this task in this life he will be reincarnated so as to continue his work in another body. The Hasidim shared the intense Messianic yearning which was current in eastern Europe in the eighteenth century, particularly in the wake of the commotions caused by the episode of Shabbetai Zvi a century earlier. The famous Hasid Levi Yitzhak of Berdichev is even said to have torn up the document announcing that his son's wedding was to take place in Berdichev, furiously exclaiming to the scribe that he should write, 'The marriage will take place in Jerusalem, unless the Messiah has not yet come, in which case the ceremony will be performed in Berdichev.' The founder of Hasidism, the Baal Shem Tov, is said to have described how he once ascended to the hall of the Messiah, and asked him when he would come. The reply was that when the Baal Shem Tov's teachings were thoroughly spread in the world, then all the 'shells' trapping the divine sparks would be ended and the era of salvation would begin. In a certain sense, however, Hasidism also provided a counterbalance to Messianism, since the Hasidic ideal of *devekut*, 'cleaving' (to God) could be achieved in the here-and-now, and some Hasidic texts use the classical Messianic term 'redemption' of the personal redemption of the individual soul.

Hasidism represents the last flowering of the medieval eschatological tradition. Its beliefs still have power to move people today, but already by the early nineteenth century the influence of the Enlightenment was compelling some Jews to reassess the traditional ideas. Enlightenment thought was hostile both to the supernaturalism and to the particularism which were such strong features of the traditional beliefs. Especially in western Europe and America, new interpretations of the traditional material evolved in the nineteenth century as part of the wider effort to adapt Judaism to the modern age.

In the area of beliefs about survival after death and the life of the Coming Age the developments were relatively restrained. These were in any case among the most fluid and nebulous of Jewish beliefs, and since they had few or no practical, halakhic repercussions they did not become a focus for outspoken controversy or dramatic reassessment. The belief in the immortality of the soul survived virtually intact, indeed it seems to have been strengthened as belief in bodily resurrection declined. The Pittsburgh Platform of 1885 probably speaks not only for the Reform rabbinate but for many other Jews as well: 'We reassert the doctrine of Judaism, that the soul of man is immortal, grounding this belief on the divine nature of the human spirit, which forever finds bliss in righteousness and misery in wickedness. We reject as ideas not rooted in Judaism the belief both in bodily resurrection and in Gehenna and Eden (hell and paradise), as abodes for everlasting punishment or reward.' On the belief in the Coming Age, which was so central in Rabbinic Judaism, the Pittsburgh Platform had nothing to say at all. It is true that some thinkers have had difficulty in dismissing so briskly the belief in resurrection, which was so important in the past, but most Jews seem to have been happy to discard it, or at least to treat it with a certain agnosticism. The reformed liturgies have eliminated explicit references to resurrection from the prayer book, or replaced them by blander allusions to 'renewal' or 'eternal life'.

It is in the area of the Messianic hope that the most significant reappraisal has taken place. Two distinct trends can be discerned here, both founded on a this-worldly interpretation of redemption and viewing it as something which can be attained by man through his own efforts, but differing on the assessment of the national ingredient in the traditional beliefs. The first trend, which has come to be associated with Reform but was in fact shared by the various modernist tendencies, stresses the universalism of the prophetic visions; the second, which bore fruit eventually in Zionism, puts a positive stress on nationalism and declares that the Jews must first and foremost redeem themselves.

The religious modernists tended to insist that Jewish identity had always been a matter of a spiritual bond. 'Land and soil', S. R. Hirsch, the spokesman of Orthodoxy, declared, 'were never Israel's bond of union.' The mission of the Jewish people was to spread the knowledge of God and the moral and religious values of Judaism to all mankind. From this standpoint, dispersion is not to be equated with exile: it is not an obstacle but an aid to the achievement of worldwide redemption. This attitude has its roots in antiquity (one ancient rabbi likens God to a farmer, who scatters his seed so as to bring in a richer harvest); in modern times it can be traced to the historical philosophy of Nachman Krochmal (1785–1840). The Israelites were chosen to be 'a kingdom of priests and a holy people': like the priests of old they had no share in the distribution of territory but were called to minister to all. The social integration arising from the emancipation could be seen as a kind of homecoming, removing the barriers between Jew and Gentile, and enabling both to work together for the kingdom of God, the reign of justice and peace, on earth. The Pittsburgh Platform encapsulates both the positive and the negative aspects of this idea:

We recognize in the modern era of universal culture of heart and intellect the approach of the realization of Israel's great Messianic hope for the establishment of the kingdom of truth, justice and peace among all men. We consider ourselves no longer a nation but a religious community, and therefore expect neither a return to Palestine, nor a sacrificial worship under the administration of the sons of Aaron, nor the restoration of any of the laws concerning the Jewish state.

We acknowledge that the spirit of broad humanity of our age is our ally in the fulfilment of our mission, and therefore we extend the hand of fellowship to all who co-operate with us in the establishment of the reign of truth and righteousness among men.

The hopeful universalism of this declaration, issued shortly after the first Russian pogroms and fifty years before the Nuremberg racial laws in Germany, has been severely tested by the course of subsequent history, and few Jews today would subscribe to it in its entirety, but the underlying approach is still influential.

The second trend may be first discerned in the writings of two eastern European rabbis, Zvi Hirsch Kalischer of Posen (1795–1874) and Judah Alkalai of Sarajevo (1798–1878). They were traditionalists whose observation of early European national movements (in Poland and Greece respectively) suggested to them the possibility of a Jewish nationalism. 'The beginning of the Redemption', Kalischer wrote in 1836, 'will come through natural causes by human effort and by the will of the governments to gather the scattered of Israel into the Holy Land.' His practical proposals for the ingathering of exiles, the restoration of sacrificial worship, and the revival of the agricultural laws regarded as binding only in the Holy Land serve to give some historical perspective to the blank rejection of these ideas in the Pittsburgh Platform. They were also opposed by other religious traditionalists, who maintained the old rabbinic prohibition on 'hastening the end', and insisted that redemption would come about in God's good time through his own supernatural intervention. Meanwhile Moses Hess (1812–75), an early socialist activist, was approaching the question of Jewish nationalism from a different background. Hess was dissatisfied with the assimilationism which was so prevalent among German Jewry, and to which he felt that neither Orthodoxy nor Reform, with their inherent denial of Jewish nationalism, could provide an answer. The essence and goal of Judaism, he argued, could not be identified with humanitarianism: humanitarianism is the blossom, nationalism is the root.

In the course of the nineteenth century Jewish nationalism became increasingly a secular, even anti-religious, political movement, and it came under attack not only from religious modernists and traditionalists (from their very different standpoints) but from many more moderate religious Jews who feared that it was substituting secular for religious values. Nevertheless, the various national movements attracted a large following, and it is interesting to notice that despite a strong secular bias the language of Jewish Messianism was never entirely discarded. Indeed, some religious thinkers have gone so far as to equate the sufferings of Jewry under Nazism with the 'birthpangs of the Messiah', and to see in the subsequent creation of the state of Israel the dawn of the Messianic era. Even the Israeli Declaration of Independence, although framed in secular terms, proclaims that 'the State of Israel will be open for Jewish immigration and for the Ingathering of Exiles' and 'will be based on freedom, justice and peace as envisaged by the prophets of Israel'. And the

Declaration concludes with these words: 'We appeal to the Jewish people throughout the Diaspora to rally round the Jews of the Land of Israel in the tasks of immigration and upbuilding and to stand by them in the great struggle for the realization of the age-old dream—the redemption of Israel.'

Epilogue: The Crisis of Contemporary Judaism

It should be clear by now that it is very hard, if not impossible, to give a simple account of Judaism in our time. Two hundred years ago, at the dawn of the modern period, it would have been possible to find considerable agreement about the basic nature and distinctive characteristics of Judaism. This agreement should not be exaggerated: even then Judaism presented different faces in different places, and the beginnings of the fundamental changes which were eventually to transform the Jewish world are clearly visible, at least with the benefit of hindsight. But it would have been easy enough to point to a relatively homogeneous tradition and say, 'This is Judaism.' Today this is no longer possible. The tradition is still there, but the unity has gone. There is no longer a widely-accepted yardstick against which any particular belief or practice, any sect or ideology, can be measured. There are many different expressions of Judaism, each claiming authenticity for itself but none recognized as definitively authentic by the others.

The present situation is the result, of course, of far-reaching historical changes, which have left their mark on Christianity as well. The world has changed almost beyond recognition in the past two centuries, and it would be astonishing if Judaism had stood still in that time. But beyond the general political, social, intellectual and religious upheavals, the Jews have been called to face certain historical challenges which have affected them in a special way. In the first place they have been physically uprooted from their old homelands, and had to create a new life in very different conditions. No less disorienting than this process of physical uprooting has been the social uprooting resulting from the breaking down of the old ghetto walls and the need to adjust to life in an open society. Thirdly, the Nazi holocaust has destroyed not only a large part of the Jewish world but the self-confidence which had begun to be built up in the face of the earlier challenges to Jewish existence. And, finally, the establishment of the state of Israel in 1948 has brought the need to adjust to yet another new reality, which has had a profound effect on the life of Jews everywhere.

Migration is an unsettling process. Jews are no strangers to migration, in fact it is a deeply-rooted feature of the Jewish historical experience. But that knowledge does not make the anxieties and practical difficulties easier to cope with. The actual experience of Jewish migrants is similar to that of all migrants. There is a period of uncertainty and of adjustment which may last over several generations: there are problems of acceptance in a new society, and a certain nostalgia for a lost past. And for most there is also the struggle simply to survive, driving other concerns into the background. Many Jewish migrants have been refugees from oppression, and this has coloured their attitudes: to their other problems has been added a feeling of rejection, and perhaps a memory of nightmare ordeals.

Even those Jews who have not made a physical move have had, like the immigrants and refugees, to adjust over a period of a few generations to a different society, in which nothing is the same as it was before. At the root of the changes is political emancipation. In the old ghetto, Jews were not fully citizens of the countries in which they lived. They had no real responsibility to the state, and they were excluded from participation in its government and administration. On the other hand the Jewish community enjoyed a high degree of self-government. Within the community the rabbis exercised real power, and Jewish law functioned as a living system. As a result of political emancipation, the Jews were integrated into the structure of the modern state. They acquired all the responsibilities and obligations of citizenship, but at the cost of losing their own institutions. The rabbis lost their political power, and Jewish law became in effect a voluntary discipline, reduced in scope to ritual and parochial concerns. These changes raised profound problems about the character of the Jewish community in the modern age, the authority of the Jewish leadership, and the role of Jewish law.

Political emancipation led to social integration. In the old ghetto, the Jews were isolated from the surrounding society. They had no need to question or justify their Jewish identity: it was a given fact of life. They were isolated physically, but they were also isolated culturally and intellectually. The opportunities open to them were severely limited: they were limited in their choice of home, marriage partner and career, and their intellectual horizons were limited by their lack of access to non-Jewish educational institutions. The gradual removal of these various barriers resulted in an enormous opening up of opportunities and mental horizons, but the new-found freedom had a disorienting effect, and raised many problems for the individual and for Jewish society as a whole. No longer protected by the ghetto walls against the influence of the surrounding culture, many Jews came to question the values and institutions inherited from the past.

Coming on top of the other upheavals, the traumatic experience of the Nazi nightmare was even more unsettling. The Nazis began by challenging and reversing the process of emancipation and integration: the Jews in Nazi Germany were deprived of their citizenship and the protection of the law, driven out of the army, the administration and the professions, and segregated from the rest of society. This reversal of modern historical processes called into question for many Jews the very possibility of a real normalization in the political and social status of the Jews of Europe. The subsequent deportations and mass-killings, highlighting the helplessness of the Jews and the depth of popular antisemitism, seemed to confirm the arguments of those who doubted whether integration were desirable or possible. But if the catastrophe of the Nazi holocaust undermined the faith in progress, it also undermined traditional religious faith. After the disaster, it seemed to many that nothing could be the same again. Gradually the process of adjustment was resumed, but in a grimmer and less optimistic mood. If there is one positive outcome, it is the beginning of a serious attempt to confront the historical causes of antisemitism, and notably the initiation of a real dialogue between Christians and Jews dedicated to the eradication of prejudice and the prevention of the recurrence of such an appalling outbreak of intolerance.

The creation of a Jewish state in Israel has done a great deal to overcome the gloomy pessimism caused by the holocaust. It has given Jews the world over a new sense of purpose and confidence. But it, too, has brought further upheavals in its train and a further need for adjustment. A Jewish state, with its own flag and army and national anthem, is something new and unknown. This new reality poses problems for those Jews who live in the Jewish state and also for those who live outside it. For those who live in Israel there are questions about Jewish identity which are different from those faced by Jews in other countries: does Israeli identity serve to define Jewish identity? If so, what is the status of the non-Jewish minorities in Israel? What is the validity of the traditional rabbinic definitions of Jewish identity? And what is the relationship between Israeli Jewish identity and the rather different Jewish identity of Jews in the diaspora? Or, if Israeli identity is something different from Jewish identity, what is the relationship between the two for Israeli Jews? And the concept of a Jewish state raises questions too about the status of Jewish religion and traditional Jewish values within the state. Should Judaism be the established religion of the state, and what should be the status of the religious minorities? Should the state be governed (wholly or partly) by Jewish law? Or, if there is a conflict between Jewish law and the law of the state, how is it to be resolved? Should the policies of the state embody Jewish ethical values, and how would this affect foreign policy, domestic economic policies, or the treatment of minorities? And is it the role of the state to promote Jewish religious observance and institutions, or should individual Jews in Israel have the same freedoms as Jews enjoy in other democracies? These are difficult questions which have given rise to heated debate. But no less difficult are the questions facing Jews outside Israel: what are the implications for their own Jewish identity of the existence of a Jewish state in Israel? How does it affect their loyalty to their own country, particularly in a case of conflict or even open war? Do Jews in the diaspora owe a special loyalty to Israel, and if they do does it extend to the specific policies of particular Israeli governments? Does the existence of Israel invalidate Jewish existence in the diaspora? Is there an obligation on all Jews to settle in Israel? Should the diaspora see itself as a kind of extension of Israel? These questions, too, have been strenuously debated, and no clear answers have yet emerged.

As a result of all these far-reaching changes the whole Jewish world is caught up in a process of re-evaluation and adjustment. Such a process of adjustment gives rise to many anxieties, prominent among which are worries about assimilation. What kind of culture, what kind of values, are parents to hand on to their children? Should they try to perpetuate the culture and values they themselves grew up with, or should they help their children to make themselves at home in the society in which they live? The answer, almost inevitably, is some kind of compromise.

Assimilation operates at different levels. It may be relatively superficial, or it may be confined to certain contexts of life. But in general, unless some kind of accommodation is reached, it tends to spread its influence gradually to all aspects of life and thought. A minority community may well safeguard its identity by agreeing (consciously or tacitly) to impose certain limits on this influence. This can be done most effectively when the community is isolated from the surrounding environment. When a minority adopts the language of the majority and is integrated within the wider educational system, it is difficult if not impossible to prevent a gradual but far-reaching assimilation to the prevailing lifestyle and patterns of thought.

Assimilation is not a new experience for Jews. Many deeply-rooted Jewish beliefs and practices were originally derived from the surrounding culture. The Yiddish language, to which many Ashkenazi Jews are still deeply attached, derives from the German adopted by Jews in medieval Germany, and likewise the Ladino or Judeo-Spanish of the Sephardim is a reminder that the Jews of medieval Spain spoke the language of the country. But in the Middle Ages the social isolation of the Jews imposed its own limits on assimilation. Jews had their own schools and even their own quarters in the towns, and this helped them to preserve their own identity and culture even as a scattered minority.

Emancipation and social integration, coupled with mass migration, have made it more difficult to resist the pressures to assimilate. In the face of this pressure, some groups of Jews have opted for the voluntary isolation of the 'new ghetto', reconstructing their own tightly-knit communities in which the old patterns of life and thought are preserved and external influences, so far as possible, are excluded. This is one extreme reaction, and of course there is an opposite extreme: total assimilation, with the abandonment of any attachment to a distinctively Jewish identity or lifestyle.

Between these two extremes there lies a whole range of possible compromises, and in the preceding chapters we have had occasion to explore some of the more obvious forms that such compromise has taken. In most countries where Jews live (with the major exception of Israel) assimilation means assimilation to a secularized Christian society, that is a society originally founded on Christian ideas and institutions, but in which these ideas and institutions no longer have the central role they had in the past. Such a society is not exceptionally threatening to a minority such as the Jews, who share many of its basic assumptions, and on whom it imposes very few unacceptable demands. In these circumstances a good deal of superficial assimilation is possible without appearing to threaten the essential character of the Jewish community. Indeed a certain amount of assimilation appears desirable, if the Jews are to be socially integrated in the society in which they live, and if they are to avail themselves of the opportunities which this society freely offers them. But nevertheless there are certain areas of conflict, there are certain pressures to conform, and there is a danger of an insidious, subtle influence on Jewish ways of thinking and behaving.

What are the limits of permissible assimilation, and what specific kinds of assimilation are desirable, tolerable, or unacceptable? These are questions on which there is no general agreement. Different attempts to answer them have given rise, as we have already observed, to a great deal of diversity in forms of Jewish identity and lifestyle. In an atmosphere of uncertainty and anxiety they have also given rise to deep divisions and antagonisms. But the diversity and the divisions take different forms in different places.

Israel, for example, is the peculiar battleground of religious traditionalism and Jewish secularism in their most extreme forms. The origins of this confrontation, which often hits the headlines with its violent demonstrations, are to be sought in conflicting images of Israel, and in different types of European immigration. The early Zionist settlers were mainly (although not exclusively) secularists, and the principal aim of Zionism was to establish a Jewish National Home (a country the Jews could call their own). But before the Zionists arrived there were already long-established communities of religious Jews, concentrated particularly in Jerusalem and the other 'holy cities' of Safed, Tiberias and Hebron, whose motivation was religious and who looked to Israel as the Holy Land. The religious Jews on the whole held themselves aloof from Zionism and opposed the creation of the Jewish state. The religious sector in Israel today is itself deeply divided. It includes the Yiddish-speaking, anti-Zionist ultra-traditionalists such as the 'Guardians of the City', who maintain a ghetto existence within the confines of the Jewish state; the Agudat Israel, a political party with a more moderate anti-Zionist stance which co-operates with the state in the furtherance of its own aims; and religious Zionists, many of whom support the National Religious Party, which has participated actively in successive government coalitions. The religious sector maintains its own schools and institutes of higher learning, and jealously preserves its own rights and privileges. But it also attempts, where it can, to extend traditionalist religious observances to the country as a whole. For example, it has effectively blocked moves to introduce civil marriage, and has thus kept control of Jewish marriages in the hands of the rabbinic courts, while preventing marriage between Jews and non-Jews. The many other areas of concern include the definition of Jewish identity, Sabbath observance, *kashrut*, abortion and postmortem examinations, pornography and mixed bathing. The traditionalists have also used their strength to block the advance of religious modernism in Israel. The secular majority has made many concessions, and on the whole has preserved the existing compromises in the interests of peace, but there is considerable resentment, and mounting pressure to reduce the power and influence of the religious sector and in particular to institute civil marriage. A result of this history of conflict is a marked polarization between the religious and the secular sectors of the population. Religion is identified with traditionalism, and the public image of religion is very largely negative.

The sudden and massive immigration into Israel of Jews from many different parts of the world, the dramatic and highly symbolic 'ingathering of exiles', has introduced another sort of conflict, between 'western' and 'oriental' Jews. Jews of different origins and cultures have co-existed side by side in many countries, but the unique history and character of Israel has given rise to particular tensions, which appear to challenge the fundamental conception of the unity of the Jewish people.

In the largest centre of Judaism, the United States, the situation is completely different. Here both traditionalism and secularism are less militant. Most Jews are attached to synagogues belonging to one or other of the modernist tendencies, and in general it is religious rather than political institutions which provide the focus for allegiance. Reform Judaism, which a century ago was the dominant trend in America, has been overtaken

numerically by Conservatism, while Orthodoxy has experienced
a striking upsurge in recent decades, partly as a result of a successful effort to found private religious schools. Pluralism, in
keeping with the general American ethos, has come to be widely
recognized as a positive virtue, and the various tendencies have
achieved a large measure of practical co-operation. Institu-
tionally, the denominational labels are as strong as ever, but on a
personal level they often count for little, and there have even been
some cases of synagogues of different trends merging. Traditionally, it is the Reform and Conservative sectors which have
been the most vocal and articulate, but Orthodoxy now seems to
be finding its voice. One of the issues it is beginning to face
squarely is the precise relationship between modernist Orthodoxy
and the various expressions of traditionalism. In fact there is a
tendency to bring them all under the collective designation of
'Orthodoxy', although this involves recognizing a certain pluralism within Orthodoxy itself. The consequences of this tendency, which represents a concerted reaction against the more
radical modernism of Reform and Conservatism, have not yet
been fully worked out; at present there is still a good deal of
polemic from the traditional sector directed against modern
Orthodoxy.

A fundamental issue which divides the various trends is the
question of observance. Faced with a situation in which the
general standards of observance are very low (a survey of New
York Jews in 1981 found that only about a third lit Sabbath
candles or bought kosher meat, while another third never attended
synagogue services), the Reform and Conservative rabbinate have
tended to respond by shifting the emphasis from liberalization
towards greater discipline and commitment, while Orthodoxy
tends to react by 'building fences round the Torah', that is,
making the Halakhah itself stricter. Although some Orthodox
rabbis have proposed that Orthodoxy ought to be influencing
Conservative Judaism in the direction of stricter observance, it
could be argued that Conservatism has exercised a stronger influence on Orthodoxy: not, as many Conservative rabbis would
wish, by strengthening its liberal tendency, but on the contrary by
encouraging a reaction in the direction of rigidity. This in turn
strengthens the hand of those Conservatives who maintain that
no compromise with Orthodoxy is possible, while encouraging

the rapprochement between modern Orthodoxy and traditionalism. The outcome would seem to be a realignment in American Judaism, with the main dividing line separating Reform Judaism and Conservatism on the one hand from Orthodoxy and traditionalism on the other. (This situation has already been reached in Britain.)

With Judaism currently in a state of evident flux, it is hard to offer any generalizations or predictions for the future. The main problem facing the leadership of all the different groups is to come up to terms with the question of Jewish identity in the open society—not just the technical question of the definition of Jewish identity, but the wider questions of content and expression. Assimilation and intermarriage on a large scale and over a long period of time have made the traditional definition of Jewish identity based on birth very difficult to administer in a sensible and consistent way, and in a way which does not seem exclusive. There are many mixed families, with technically non-Jewish children of Jewish parents and non-Jewish parents of Jewish children. There are many Jews with little or no Jewish upbringing, and also non-Jews with a strong attachment to Judaism. This is a novel situation, and for a religion based as strongly on the family and the home as Judaism has traditionally been it poses a serious challenge which the traditional institutions have not yet found a way of facing up to. In fact the traditional strength of the Jewish home is being eroded in the face of competition from the synagogue and the school, which are the main focus of the effort to keep the next generation Jewish and to increase the content of Jewish expression. This is another challenge which is difficult to meet. Nor is it easy, in the open society, to attract the best talents into the service of the Jewish community as rabbis and educators, or to ensure that Jewish children receive a Jewish education, even of the most elementary kind.

The existence of Jewish secularism, that is, Jewish identity and commitment combined with apathy or antagonism towards religion, is another novel situation which has hardly been recognized, let alone faced up to. It is only in Israel so far that secularism has come out into the open and raised its voice; but there is no doubt that Jewish secularism is a widespread phenomenon. It raises problems both for the secularists themselves and for the religious leadership. For the secularists there is the problem of expressing and perpetuating a Jewish commitment which is divorced from religion. For the religious leadership there is the problem of how far secular Judaism is to be recognized as an authentic version of Judaism for our time, and also the subtler problem of recognizing and responding to the invasion by secular values and habits of the religious domain itself. The synagogue, for example, which in the diaspora has become the main focus for Jewish identification and activity, is tending to become secularized as a community centre, offering a variety of activities among which religious services may occupy only a part, and in some cases a minor part at that. This change reflects the fact that for many Jews now, perhaps the majority, religion no longer occupies a central place in their lives, and yet they feel a need to be publicly identified with a Jewish community, to mix socially with other Jews, and to pass on some kind of Jewish commitment to their children.

In this context it is worth mentioning the special problems facing Judaism in the third-largest centre of the Jewish world, the Soviet Union. Cut off from regular contact with the rest of the Jewish world, and particularly from its major centres in America and Israel, and deprived of facilities for religious education and worship (there are only some sixty synagogues in the whole Soviet Union, half of them situated in the Caucasus and Central Asia, far from the main areas of Jewish population), Soviet Jews are not even free to develop their own forms of secular Jewish identity and culture without the most intense struggles with the apparatus of the state. Amid all the anxieties about Jewish survival in the aftermath of the holocaust, the plight of Soviet Jewry is a cause of special concern.

What is the place of religion in Jewish life? In the past its influence was all-encompassing. In today's situation only a small minority feel able to lead a 'fully Jewish life'. This minority consists, on the one hand, of the traditionalists and some members of modernist communities, and on the other hand of the professional leadership of the modernist communities, who must sometimes feel that they have become the vicarious representatives of the Judaism of their members. Should Judaism be dictated from above, or should it also be responsive to pressures from below? This is an old question, but in the context of the low level of religious observance today it takes on a new turn. The rabbis may try to influence their congregants by their teaching and preaching and by their personal example, but they are powerless to compel compliance. Should they then turn a blind eye to neglect of the observances, should they stigmatize their less observant members as sinners, or should they reassess the level of observance that they demand, and perhaps even apply the new standards to their own behaviour?

It is partly in response to this problem that the various kinds of Jewish modernism have evolved in the way they have, and each would no doubt offer a different solution. But the basic problem remains, and so does the question of the relative emphasis on law and ritual in Jewish life, as compared to other activities such as study or social responsibility. There are other questions too, such as the balance between wholehearted devotion and formal observance, or the demand for ethical behaviour going beyond the letter of the law. These are questions to which different answers have been suggested, but perhaps more important than any of them is the question of tolerance of dissent, and a willingness to admit that there are many different ways of being Jewish, none of which perhaps is completely right or wrong.

There are two further questions in the area of religion which arise out of the contemporary situation. One is the place of women in Jewish religious life. As we have seen, traditional Judaism offered only a limited role to women. Contemporary Jewish traditionalism maintains this stance, and even Orthodoxy has made very few concessions. How long such an attitude can be perpetuated in an age of sexual equality remains to be seen, but already there is a growing Jewish feminist movement which challenges the traditional arguments and seeks a greater measure of participation for women in the life of the religious community, as well as the reform of those areas of the religious law which discriminate in favour of men.

The second question is the relationship between Judaism and other religions. Judaism has never presented itself as the exclusive path to salvation, and consequently it has never concerned itself greatly with other religions, except in so far as it has felt a need to defend itself against aggressive polemic and missionary activity. In the present situation, however, which favours a *rapprochement* between different religions, and in which Christians, in particular, are seeking a closer relationship with Judaism on the basis of understanding and dialogue rather than conversionism, many Jews have felt called on to extend a hand of friendship to other religious groups, to participate in joint activities, and even in some circumstances to pool resources and work together for specific causes. This change, too, has demanded a great effort of adjustment, and it has met with some resistance. There may be barriers of prejudice which will need to be broken down in the future.

So far we have been concerned in the main with questions and problems, and there is no doubt that they are many. But it would be wrong to conclude without stressing some of the positive aspects of the contemporary situation. Despite all the upheavals, and the devastating calamity of the holocaust, the Jewish world has emerged in many ways strengthened by the trials of its latest history. The gloomy predictions which have been voiced for more than a century have not been fulfilled. Neither the open enemy of antisemitism nor the subtler enemy of assimilation has succeeded in ridding the world of the Jews or crushing their spirit. On the contrary, the will to survive is stronger than ever. Jews have responded to the challenge of freedom by seizing the new opportunities and adapting to the new situations. After a long period of extreme uncertainty and excessive compromise, there is now a realization that a free society can allow minorities the freedom to be themselves. Instead of maintaining a low profile and attempting to merge unobtrusively into their surroundings, young Jews today in America and elsewhere are proudly vaunting their Jewishness, and seeking new ways to express it. Jewish studies are being introduced into the university curriculum, and there is a positive appreciation of Jewish culture and the Jewish contribution to civilization. Even in the Soviet Union, against the most daunting obstacles, there is an exciting rediscovery of the Jewish cultural heritage. It is true that Jewishness is not the same thing as Judaism: it suggests an ethnic rather than a religious commitment, in keeping with a wider contemporary trend. But there are signs of a religious revival, too, including a heightened awareness of the spiritual richness of traditional Jewish religion, with its emotional fervour and its wealth of ritual and mystical imagery.

In all this renewal of vitality an important role must be ascribed to the phenomenon of Israel. The establishment of the Jewish state, following swiftly on the nightmarish ordeal of the Nazi era, offered more than reassurance and a boost to shattered self-confidence. It reestablished the legendary link between the people of Israel and the Land of Israel. It provided a concrete and visible focus for Jewish identity, and united the Jews of the world in shared aspirations and dedicated effort. Young Jews from assimilated backgrounds flocked to Israel, and stayed to settle or came back inspired with a devotion to Jewish ideals which would have been barely imaginable a few generations ago. And Jews who were born and grew up in the Jewish state have had the privilege of knowing what it is to be naturally and unselfconsciously Jewish, with no tension of dual loyalties or pressures of minority existence. Many of them, particularly after the dramatic reunification of Jerusalem in 1967, have also experienced a religious awakening and a renewal of interest in the spiritual potential of Judaism. But for Jews everywhere Israel has become a symbol, of the life of the Jewish people, of unity within diversity, and, above all, of hope.

Further Reading

General Reference

Encyclopaedia Judaica (16 vols., Jerusalem, 1971-2)

Chapter 1

Baron, S. W., *Social and Religious History of the Jews*, 2nd edn. (18 vols. to date, New York and Philadelphia, 1952-)

de Lange, N., *Atlas of the Jewish World* (Oxford and New York, 1984)

Grayzel, S., *A History of the Contemporary Jews* (Philadelphia, 1960)

Mendes-Flohr, P. R., and Reinharz, J. (eds.), *The Jew in the Modern World: a Documentary History* (Oxford, 1980)

Chapter 2

Blau, J. L., *Modern Varieties of Judaism* (New York, 1966)

Bulka, R. P. (ed.), *Dimensions of Orthodox Judaism* (New York, 1983)

Davis, M., *The Emergence of Conservative Judaism* (Philadelphia, 1963)

Plaut, W. G., *The Growth of Reform Judaism* (New York, 1965)

Rotenstreich, N., *Tradition and Reality: the Impact of History on Modern Jewish Thought* (New York, 1972)

Chapter 3

Donin, H. L., *To Pray as a Jew* (New York, 1980)

Idelsohn, A. Z., *Jewish Liturgy and Its Development* (New York, 1932)

Jacobs, L., *Hasidic Prayer* (London, 1973)

Millgram, A. E., *Jewish Worship* (Philadelphia, 1971)

Chapter 4

Bamberger, B. J., *The Bible: a Modern Jewish Approach*, 2nd edn. (New York, 1963)

Casper, B. M., *Introduction to Jewish Bible Commentary* (London and New York, 1960)

Hertz, J. H. (ed.), *The Pentateuch and Haftorahs*, 2nd edn. (London, 1966)

Jacobs, L., *Jewish Biblical Exegesis* (New York, 1973)

Sandmel, S., *The Hebrew Scriptures: an Introduction to their Literature and Religious Ideas*, 2nd edn. (New York, 1978)

Chapter 5

Berkovits, E., *Not in Heaven: the Nature and Function of Halakhah* (New York, 1983)
Elon, M. (ed.), *The Principles of Jewish Law* (Jerusalem, 1975)
Freehof, S. B., *The Responsa Literature* (New York, 1955)
Klein, I., *A Guide to Jewish Religious Practice* (New York, 1979)

Chapter 6

Bernfeld, S., *The Foundation of Jewish Ethics*, revised edn. (New York, 1968)
Fox, M. (ed.), *Modern Jewish Ethics: Theory and Practice* (Columbus, Ohio, 1975)
Jakobovits, I., *Jewish Medical Ethics* (New York, 1967)
Spero, S., *Morality, Halakha and the Jewish Tradition* (New York, 1981)

Chapter 7

Rabinowicz, H., *The World of Hasidism* (London, 1970)
Scholem, G., *Major Trends in Jewish Mysticism*, 3rd edn. (New York, 1954)
—— *Kabbalah* (Jerusalem, 1974)

Chapter 8

Guttmann, J., *Philosophies of Judaism*, tr. D. W. Silverman (Philadelphia and London, 1964)
Jacobs, L., *A Jewish Theology* (London, 1973)
Katz, S. T. (ed.), *Jewish Philosophers* (Jerusalem, 1975)
Kohler, K., *Jewish Theology* (New York, 1918, repr. New York, 1968)

Chapter 9

Hertzberg, A. (ed.), *The Zionist Idea: a Historical Analysis and Reader* (New York, 1959)
Scholem, G., *The Messianic Idea in Judaism* (New York, 1971)
Silver, A. H., *A History of Messianic Speculation in Israel* (New York, 1927)

Index